PUBLISHED by PARABLES
Earthly Stories with a Heavenly Meaning

Messenger of the Lord

By
Chris Hamman

PUBLISHED by PARABLES
Earthly Stories with a Heavenly Meaning

MESSENGER OF THE LORD
Chris Hamman

Published By Parables
March, 2019

All Rights Reserved. No part of this book may be reproduced or utilized in any form or by any means, electronic or mechanical, including photocopying, recording, or by any information storage and retrieval system, without permission in writing from the author.

ISBN 978-1-945698-92-7
Printed in the United States of America

Readers should be aware that Internet Web sites offered as citations and/or sources for further information may have been changed or disappeared between the time this was written and the time it is read.

Messenger of the Lord

By
Chris Hamman

PUBLISHED by PARABLES
Earthly Stories with a Heavenly Meaning

†

1Ti 3:15 but if I tarry long, that thou mayest know how men ought to behave themselves in the house of God, which is the church of the living God, the pillar and ground of the truth.

Chris Hamman

As the early morning sun slowly rises over the horison, its golden rays gently dissolving the mist upon the lake, revealing the beauty of creation, it also gently but purposefully reveals the dangers lurking in dark places so that we may not be caught unawares. Shadows on the murky looking water start to disappear as the rays of the sun penetrates its deep secrets. The word of God likewise shines forth both warnings, admonishing's and encouragements as well as the beauty of the Lord, helping us to navigate the way before us to the glory of the Son. My prayer is that this book will reveal the message it contains in like manner so that the reader may find the message palatable and worthy to be meditated upon.

INDEX

PREFACE 6

INTRODUCTION.. 9

LOVING THE LORD... 12

HAGGAI THE PROPHET AND THE CONDITION OF THE
HOUSE OF THE LORD 16

AS SWEET AS HONEY... 24

ADDRESSING ANGELS... 30

GRIPPED BY THE LORD... 32

A PRAYING BRIDE.. 40

CLOTHING THE BRIDE.. 46

THE BEAUTIFUL BRIDE 52

WALKING IN THE SPIRIT... 66

THE ARK OF THE LORD.. 72

ENTERING HEAVEN... 76

THE WILL OF GOD.. 81

THE WILL OF GOD PART 2... 85

PREPARING OUR HEARTS... 89

JOHN AND THE ANGELS.. 95

GOLDEN LAMPSTANDS.. 101

THE CHURCH..107

REVELATION 2 verse 1.. 113

THE BEGINNING.. 119

REFERENCE MATERIAL... 120

PREFACE

Joh 1:23 He said, I am *the voice of one crying in the wilderness, (KJV)*.

Walking in the shadows of the Namibian desert's formidable sand dunes can be a scary experience as they seem to change shape making it difficult if not impossible to find ones way back by them. Experienced guides will tell you to not venture into the Namib Desert alone and to backtrack using your own tracks made in the sand before the wind covers them. The sand dunes are the same ones the explorers of many years ago traversed that we are able to climb today. Yet they seem to have a different shape as the earth rotates, changing their image and shadow and by walking 10 or more yards on.

My description of the dune may vary from yours due to our different vantage points and time we visited them. We may be describing the same dune although we have a different perspective of its shape. Our communication with each other will maybe reveal much more of the enormity of the dune than just our own perception.

My message could be from a different vantage point of the bible but it is the same bible you may hold in your hand. The message birthed in my heart of what you are about to read is to bring my perspective to Christian spiritual leaders' attention, in a most dramatic way, of how precious they are, their deep value to the

Lord and what I hear Him asking of them today. The desire is to stir them spiritually and personally to go further, go deeper, to search and experience the joy of finding more of the Truth than ever before. By indulging in looking from my vantage point the desire is for you the reader to become a lover of God our Father and a "world changer" for the Lord right where you are right now in a new fresh baptism in His word.

A novice in computer technology phoned the help desk after purchasing a desk top PC with Windows 1.3 as its OS. The novice asked how do one switch off the machine to which the operator replied "Click on the Start button lower left of your screen" The novice immediately replied "I want to switch it off, not start it please"!! Well, you can imagine the conversation resulting from this! The fact that we need to press start to switch off is not logical at all. For someone who is a beginner or novice, the question is absolutely logical. We need some what I would call "inside knowledge" that goes beyond our existing perception and understanding. This knowledge is provided by the designer or author of the program. Scripture often confronts our human understanding with issues requiring "inside knowledge". Holy Spirit is the author therefore He needs to explain scripture that does not always seem logical to our human understanding. Argue as we may, behind the Start button is a program that switches the machine off.

Nicodemus had a big problem with the statement that he had to be born again to enter heaven! "How can you enter your mother's womb again", was his logical question.

The answer to Nicodemus of course as we know, is that Jesus was speaking of a spiritual reality and not the fleshly. The spiritual man is reborn into a spiritual relationship with his Maker. Jesus showed us how to live this spiritual life whilst still in the fleshly body.

In Acts 4 verses 8 to 21 we see that the synagogue leaders do not understand or do not want to understand what has taken place before their own eyes or were given the information from reputable sources. They spoke to recipients of healings and demonic deliverances yet they shunned the evidence. The fact that something heavenly has taken place, a whole family blessed and the nation excited did not create in them any joy but rather jealousy which, as we know leads to hate and eventually to murder (Cain murdered Abel due to jealousy) ! Many reports of His works surrounded them. Jesus was the talk of the town so to speak yet they chose not to believe.

In this book "Messenger of the Lord" I wish to share with the reader what the Lord showed me from my vantage point of scripture which I believe is a phenomenal, encouraging, heartwarming "word" for our spiritual leaders of the Church of Jesus Christ, including me the writer. I wish for the reader to keep in mind that we need "inside knowledge" when interpreting scripture. Led by the Author the Holy Spirit to specific scriptures revealing God's heart regarding the church and its leadership, I began to realise the enormity of the task that lies ahead for the church and the leaders in the church, today.

Consider the fact that Jesus asks of us to follow Him and do the same wonderful things He did and more! He said we will be able to do even greater things!!! What then happened that we are not completely following? This book is all about what the Lord requires of His church today, to realise the enormity of the trust He has bestowed in us. I am one of many who has heard Him concerning His Body on earth and have humbly penned down what I believe He is saying.

Writing this book relates to my hearts' desire that the ministers of the church become "the magnificent voice of the Lord" through constant communion with Him. As the writer of this book I must admit I am not the author of it. I believe with all my heart that what I have received is from the Lord, the Holy Spirit being the actual author. As such I believe that the Holy Spirit will guide the reader to the truth even though it is sometimes clothed in the weakness of the flesh. Reader will need some "inside knowledge" to discern what the Lord is saying.

In God's word we are asked to be like children. That is me. It asks for humbleness. I believe that is me. It says we are all sinners. Yes, that is truly me. Paul says he was the greatest of sinners. Sorry Paul but I am the greatest sinner. We are saved by grace not works. That is me also! I have nothing to show you, but Jesus. What I share is for us, for me as well. It is His word, His will and His purpose.

Cathrine Kulmann one of the greatest evangelists in America in the 1950's said of herself: "If you have never met Cathrine Kulmann, you have missed nothing". Yet hundreds of people got saved and healed in her services. All the glory belongs to Him! I paraphrase Act's 4 verse 10: "Let it be known that by the name of Jesus Christ the Nazarene who was crucifies for us, whom God raised from the dead, by that name I stand before you today". In all humbleness, knowing the weakness of the flesh, I walk like Jacob, with a limp, unable to hide my humanity and need for Him constantly.

Chris Hamman

INTRODUCTION

Rev 2:1 Unto the angel of the church of Ephesus write; These things saith he that holdeth the seven stars in his right hand, who walketh in the midst of the seven golden candlesticks;(KJV)

As this book is about the Church and its ministers I thought it necessary to consider the Builder of it as well. What plan did the Builder use and what principles or rules were applied? Not the building of brick and stone which also will require a master builder, but I am referring to the spiritual house made of people, not bricks. Yet there is so much similarities in the process of both that Peter uses the physical building (1 Peter 2 v 5) as did Jesus (Math 21 v 42) to describe this spiritual building, amongst many others.

In providing Moses with how the tabernacle is to be constructed, the bible has an elaborate detailed description of the plan provided by the Lord. Likewise the first and second temple were constructed exactly as per the instructions of the Lord. Why is this given to us in so much detail? One of the reasons I believe is that God wanted us to understand that His instructions have eternal meaning and consequences. The foundation must be laid exactly as described. There is a reason! I need not go into much detail here as I believe the reader will know this very well. What I would like the reader to understand is that God has a "plan" for His spiritual church as well. If we build according to our own understanding and plan it will violate the will of God, would it not?

In 1 Cron 15 we read that David made the mistake of carrying the ark on a brand new wagon specially made for it yet not Gods will. David wanted to show the Lord how much he revered the Ark of the Covenant and loved the Lord so He got men to make a new wagon on which nothing was carted before. Yet someone died because of David not following God's ordained will. (1 Cron. 15 v 13) We then read that when he obeyed the Lord (1Cron 15 v 2) and instructed that the Levites carry the ark, the ark arrived in Jerusalem and a new way of worship began. David had a large choir and musicians worshipping the Lord 24 hours a day 7 days a week. The ark represented the presence of God Almighty...The obedience to His will brings blessings as we read of David's successful exploits as a warrior king.

God is truly in these last days doing something new. A word from Lana Vawser also gives us a clue of what is about to be and I quote:

"Jesus then spoke to me (Lana):

"Lana, in order to enter this room, all agendas, all old wineskins and strategies must be laid down. The old wineskins and strategies were not bad, they were breathed on by Me, but now a new era has been entered into and to enter in, My people must come in empty handed, hearts open and willing to embrace change. For I have been decreeing that these are the days of Psalm 24:7-9. I, the King of Glory am about to step in and come through My people in a way never seen before, but to see with clarity the new wineskins for this era there must be a surrender to My way, to My changes and knowing things will not look the same."

"Surrender to My way"...! In His will the basics always stays the same, yet change must come! He will make a way where there is no way. This book will endeavor to highlight the revealed will of God for His church, the Bride of Chris so that what He wants to do can be done.

There are many wonderful things revealed about angels in scripture. Heavenly beings that appear and disappear. Sometimes in human form and at other times in their heavenly form, they give us a sense of heaven itself. It also informs us that there is a mighty war going on and that they are very much part of it. What impressed me which I want to share with you <u>is the obvious fact that angels are continually in the presence of God almighty.</u> They know Him, know His heart, see Him, love Him, hear Him, worship and obey Him.

Angels have been one of the phenomenon's in scripture that captures the attention of not only Christians but even more so the imagination of the secular world and the film industry. Angels appeared too many of the people mentioned in the bible and also to Jesus who was strengthened by an angel before His crucifixion. Angels are heavenly beings under the command of God Himself and they appear to fulfil the tasks of messenger, warrior and protector. They are also involved with the praise and worship in heaven, described as cherubim. Many people on earth have witnessed that they saw angels who appeared to them, sometimes physically and sometimes in dreams and visions.

Angels do not respond to human instructions or demands. They are heavenly beings and respond to God alone. (As must our spiritual leaders) They are not male or female. Jesus explained to the Sadducees that there is no more male or female but all will be like the angels in heaven. (Math 22 v 30)

This book heavily underscores the fact that church leaders are as angels (messengers) to the Lord. He wants them to be in His presence constantly. What I heard concerns all church leaders, all who are called ones. Please listen with me to the One who called.

Chris Hamman

LOVING THE LORD

Mat 22:37 Jesus said unto him, Thou shalt love the Lord thy God with all thy heart, and with all thy soul, and with all thy mind.

Joh 21:15 so when they had broken their fast, Jesus saith to Simon Peter, Simon, son of John, lovest thou me more than these?

The very first problem the Lord reveals in Revelations 2 is that there is a critical lack of "first love". This love is not the fleshly love where we say to each other "I love you", feeling great and loving towards another. This love is saying to God He is our all, our very breath and existence, our Father whom we respect and fear, the One who captured our hearts through the Beloved. This Love is of a God-kind. It is powerful, merciful, creative and joyful. This Love knows no boundaries and trusts the One who gives it. The love mentioned here is the type of childlike love that blesses and not condemns, a type of love that allows us to walk in faith and act in faith on His word. This love trusts Him unconditionally and fears no evil from anyone, that all He promised will come to pass. This is a bride to bridegroom kind of love, a sold out to the One loved (*Son 5:8 I adjure you, O daughters of Jerusalem, If ye find my beloved, That ye tell him, that I am sick from love*).

I found the following statement, amongst others, In a recent article by the leadership expert Dave Kraft (I place his full shared word with his permission as <u>Annexure A</u> that we may read the message in its context) quite relevant to the judgment Jesus makes and what I feel I should share with you the reader (Words in brackets added):

(Christian) Leaders must (first of all) guard against a ministry becoming (like) a mistress (idol). A mistress is someone who takes the place that only a wife should occupy. Ministry must never take the place of Jesus Himself in our heart and in our values. As 1 John 5:21 says, "Little children, keep yourselves from idols." The New Living Translation says, "Dear children, keep away from anything that might take God's place in your hearts." Our hearts are idol factories, and ministry, for many leaders, (can become) is the king of idols.

The Devil is out to snare Christian leaders, rendering them "ineffective or unfruitful" (2 Peter 1:8), and if he can't achieve his purposes through obvious sin, he will achieve them by taking something that is admirable and good and turning it on its ear to cause us to stumble. (End quote) If we are found to be serving men in the place of where Jesus should be in our hearts, it is idolatry — plain and simple and perhaps painful for us to admit.

We must purposefully guard against this possibility happening. We need to make every day an issue of placing and keeping Jesus as our primary focus. We need to ask for the power of Jesus through the Holy Spirit to occupy first place in our hearts. <u>He must be our First love</u>! *It may well be that ministry idolatry is an attitude, a mind-set, as opposed to an action. It begins with the way we look at things, the way we think. (Dave Kraft)*

My desire is that Christian leaders maintain or develop this intimate, personal, fellowship with the Lord, first of all as an individual worshipper of God and secondly as a leader. I desire that each who read here will focus on what the Lord is saying to each individually. We so easily direct what we learn to who we think the revelation may refer to. Please put this book down if you are convinced this book is for someone you know or some church you have visited. This book contains what I believe is a very personal word of truth and encouragement. You are key to the magnificent expansion of the Lord`s move on earth in the last days.

Dear reader, this book (I did not realise that this message would eventually become a book!) contains what I believe is a Spirit filled, prophetic word of love, encouragement and a request for a personal recommitment and possibly realignment, to us as the spiritual leaders in the church of the Lord, His bride on earth. The purpose of the Lord, it seems to me, is to revive the hearts of His sent ones, to encourage and to create a kind of worship and adoration that will flow like living waters from the heart. Something wants to explode from within you and me which has been delayed and kept secret and needs to come out, to be exposed and to influence a generation that needs the Lord more than ever before.

As mentioned before, I was led by the Spirit of the Lord to many scriptures and personal testimonies that confirmed what I heard the Lord say regarding spiritual leaders and His church, the bride of Christ. Having spent time on the mission field in Namibia and serving as deacon and elder in the church, attending many local congregations and different ministries, my commitment to and faith in the awesome role that the local churches has to play in Christian communities, deepened over the years. Quite a substantial number of Christian books formed my understanding of the word of God regarding His bride, including many personal revelations received along the way. In writing this book I have sought to share my understanding of the message to the leaders within the bride of Christ under the leadership of the Holy Spirit, passionately seeking to "wake up" personal gifting's and to encourage leaders of the flock to increase in the "walk" (minister) worthy of the Lord Jesus Christ.

The apostle Peter says, "Be sober-minded; be watchful. Your adversary the devil prowls around like a roaring lion, seeking someone to devour" (1 Peter 5:8). Our enemy can devour us through ministry by letting the ministry itself replace Jesus in our affections. Unfortunately, we are often quicker to recognize this happening in others than in our own lives.

The message I received is for His sent ones, the stars in His hand, the angels of the church (Rev. 2 v 1) The Lord loves us so much and wants us "up there" with Him. He wants us to move and bathe in His love continually. God in His mercy and kindness birthed this message over many years of ups and downs in my own spiritual life. The task of the church, apart from being a place of **worship, also needs to teach, to testify, to minister, to mentor until** the sheep become Spirit filled ministers themselves. This multiplication has not happened dramatically, as it was after the outpouring of Holy Spirit at Pentecost? Had it been true with us today, then the Lord can maybe come because we the church would have been able to bring to every living person on earth the revealed good news?

You and I have been chosen. In John 15 verse 16 we read what Jesus said: *Ye have not chosen me, but **I have chosen you, and ordained you**, that ye should go and bring forth fruit, and that your fruit should remain: that whatsoever ye shall ask of the Father in my name, he may give it you.* Please note here that Jesus says He ordained them, the apostles, to go and work in the vineyards' of the Lord. ".(*Mat 4:18 And Jesus, walking by the sea of Galilee, saw two brethren, Simon called Peter, and Andrew his brother, casting a net into the sea: for they were fishers.*
19 And he saith unto them, Follow me, and I will make you fishers of men.)
(Barnes' Commentary on John 15:16 is fully quoted in Annexure B) We will see later how this verse ties in beautifully with other scriptures and the message I received from the Lord.

What I received initially from the Lord and had me reach for "pen and paper", evolved into a more comprehensive message as He revealed His heart to me. Having this revelation of being chosen by Him personally (the leaders in the church), His love for us, our task and His desire that we love Him too, became interwoven with the calling described in the following chapters. The absolute reliance on Holy Spirit flowed naturally into the narrative of my discourse in sharing this word.

Each chapter also stands on its own, although every one of them were initiated by the core message, that the angels of the Lord must take action. In the following chapter I will explain where I found an indication of the issues the Holy Spirit is underlining with an urgency that made me meditate more and more as to the significance thereof.

Son 5:10 My beloved is white and ruddy, The chiefest among ten thousand. His head is as the most fine gold; His locks are bushy, and black as a raven. His eyes are like doves beside the waterbrooks, Washed with milk, and fitly set. His cheeks are as a bed of spices, As banks of sweet herbs: His lips are as lilies, dropping liquid myrrh. His hands are as rings of gold set with beryl: His body is as ivory work overlaid with sapphires. His legs are as pillars of marble, set upon sockets of fine gold: His aspect is like Lebanon, excellent as the cedars. His mouth is most sweet; Yea, he is altogether lovely. This is my beloved, and this is my friend, O daughters of Jerusalem.

Chris Hamman

HAGGAI THE PROPHET AND THE CONDITION

OF THE HOUSE OF THE LORD

Ye have not chosen me, but I have chosen you, <u>and ordained you,</u> that ye should go and bring forth fruit, and that your fruit should remain: that whatsoever ye shall ask of the Father in my name, he may give it you (Joh 15 verse 16).

(THE DREAM)

The writing of this book came about as a result of my overwhelming conviction that the church is not as effective as it should be and in fact "dead" to what the Lord is asking of it. I felt I may be too late. Then I had the following dream (Wednesday 5am - 12 July 2017 (Wednesday 5am - 12 July 2017)

Some years ago we had neigbours across the road from us who were both aged residents and our friends (80+ years). We have since moved to another town and haven't seen them for more than 4 years. In this dream I saw myself planting what I think was a fig tree, about 1.5 meters tall, on my plot. My neighbour, let's call him John (not his real name), was standing directly in front of the tree I had just planted and opposite to me. We had some sort of discussion and were talking when he suddenly started to keel over backwards and grabbing the tree, fell over, hitting his head against the road surface. I ran over to him and saw blood coming out of his mouth, ears and some oozing from below his head where it hit the tarmac.

My reaction in this dream was to accept that he had died and so I went for help. There were other people with me but I do not know who they were. I found his wife Mary (not her real name) at their home and told her that I have sad news, very sad news. Funny, she was the type that would panic at this point but she did not so I repeated the fact that I had very bad news and told her her husband had died.

In the dream we moved to the place where he lay and found him beginning to stand up! I was completely taken by surprise and helped him get up, We then moved to what I believe was their house whilst he was talking, obviously a little disheveled and incoherent.

Then I woke up and remembered the dream in detail. Wondering what it meant, the Lord gave me this interpretation:

The planting of the tree represents me "establishing a little new life" or a word of encouragement by I believe, this book. The fact that this man fell over showed me that the church should be upright, standing, not falling. The fact that it was an oldish person, gave me the impression the church is working with old anointing, gifts that have become stagnant It cannot uphold the church in the present challenges it faces.

My immediate acceptance that the person is dead was clearly wrong. I realised that my perceptions are faulty. The church is not dead, at least not as dead as I assumed it to be. There is still life and the ability to stand up again, even though it has taken a hard knock!

This dream also underlined the fact that the Lord will do it as I had no influence or power to raise up my neighbour. He got up by himself in the dream!!

My dear reader, I am convinced and believe that what I share with you is from God who Himself will be the personal voice to you through the messages contained in this book. As you read on, please be sensitive to the Holy Spirit as I hope and pray He may speak to you through this message I bring in all humbleness.

This dream came at a time that I was shown what the scriptures in Haggai wants to convey as a now word to the church, even though the prophet obviously refer to the rebuilding of the temple. I have often found the Lord revealing fresh revelations from the Old Testament but with a more spiritual meaning for today.

In my own personal bible, the NAS from the Lockman Foundation (Holman Bible Publishers, Nashville, USA) the summary of the book Haggai contains a very important interpretation of what the prophet Haggai was given to convey to Israel at that time and I quote: *"The prophet ruthlessly exposes the false but prevalent view that God's work is secondary and must wait for the solution of economic problems"* end quote. Haggai says it thus: *Hag 1:2 Thus speaketh the LORD of hosts, saying, This people say, The time is not come, the time that the LORD'S house should be built.* Verse 4 states: *Is it time for you, O ye, to dwell in your ceiled houses, and this house lie waste (or "desolate" as some translations state)?*

In other words, when the Lord asks us to look after the poor or to minister in some way above our means or ability, we first focus on what we have, what is in our purse or own ability. We may find there is too little resources available and then resist or refuse to help, excusing ourselves from doing what the Lord is asking of us. I have been at such a place a number of times and to my shame have disappointed my Lord. Is this not a lack of faith perhaps? Is it a view of God's will and ability to use us and provide the resource? I think so! Haggai's word from the Lord shows that the lack of resources is in fact the result of neglect, of acting and doing, by faith. Reaching out in faith is what the Lord requires from all of us. Faith is not what you have or see but what you cannot see: *Rom_8:24 For we are saved by hope: but hope that is seen is not hope: for what a man seeth, why doth he yet hope for?*

I believe the Lord is asking His bride to come searching, to come expecting, in faith, to find Him faithful and true. We need to come boldly doing His will and not counting the cost, passionately expecting divine intervention and provision for the church and ourselves. To get to grips with the word I received we need to understand the need for this awesome revelation. This the Lord showed me in Haggai specifically.

In Haggai 1 verse 4 and 9 we read that God is saying His house lies desolate (or waste). The Oxford Advanced Learners Dictionary explains this word "desolate" dramatically in terms of the Lord's use of it: "empty and without people, making you feel sad and frightened, very lonely and unhappy, without hope! Remember this is the Lord's view, not ours. Then the Lord explains what He is actually saying (My house lies desolate) in the following verses (6 to 8):

1. <u>Sowing.</u> *<u>Hag 1:6 Ye have sown much, and bring in little........</u>*

The Lord I believe is saying we throw out our nets but they bring in little fish. According to world statistics only one third of the world population are Christians. This figure may well be much lower as we know that many who profess to be followers of Jesus Christ are that only in name. The churches face a massive task ahead as the Lord is seeking the lost sheep! Is there something wrong with the net or the fishermen? Sowing is man's task and clearly we are being told our sowing is far too little and ineffective. The net is not the main problem but the sower. There are far too little sowers and those who do are sowing where rocks and weeds come up: *Mat 13:27 "And the slaves of the landowner came and said to him, 'Sir, did you not sow good seed in your field? How then does it have tares?' "And he said to them, 'An enemy has done this!'*

Pastor Reinhardt Bonke sends in prayer warriors to the areas they are to hold an outreach to ensure the word is received without the enemy being able to intervene. Witchdoctors have been saved as have known witches and many lame and sick healed through the gospel being preached. He boldly in the name of our Lord cleans the "air" and invites the local churches to join in. In fact, this pastor works with the churches in unity from the beginning.

Have we forgotten our enemy? He has not forgotten us. He rules here on earth as the bible tells us so clearly... *Joh 12:31 "Now judgment is upon this world; now the ruler of this world shall be cast out. Joh 14:30 "I will not speak much more with you, for the ruler of the world is coming, and he has nothing in Me; Joh 16:11 and concerning judgment, because the ruler of this world has been judged.*

Our nets need repair and we need to pray for more labourers. We do not pray because we lost our first love, not listening to what is most important to the Lord today. China and India as well as some other parts of the world are experiencing revival because much prayer has been made for them. How about the lost in South Africa, America, etc.? God has shifted the lost from far off in the homelands to right up to our front door. Thousands upon thousands of homeless await the good news. Too little is being done by the church?

2. <u>Eating: Hag 1 verse 6b   ".... you eat, but there is not enough to be satisfied....."</u>

I believe the Lord is referring to His word here: *Isa 55:2 "Why do you spend money for what is not bread, And your wages for what does not satisfy? Listen carefully to Me, and eat what is good, And delight yourself in abundance.*

Abundance!! Eat what is good and we will delight ourselves in the abundance of it!! Our spirit man is hungry yet we do not feed it, we ignore the hunger pains and have become used to being hungry, in fact we do not even know that we hunger.

The Lord says to His disciples: *Joh 4:32 But He said to them, "I have food to eat that you do not know about."* <u>Mat 5:6</u> *"Blessed are those who hunger and thirst for righteousness, for they shall be <u>satisfied.</u>*

When we "eat" the word of the Lord we begin to become satisfied but as with normal eating in the natural we need to constantly eat to be constantly satisfied. We have to be fed constantly, even though the food is the same food. Knowing the word of God does not mean we do not have to read it again and again. We have to!! Every one of us must spend quality time with the word of the Lords personally, not just to preach it. Sermons must come from the heart, not our minds only. That requires time spent eating the word, again and again. Thus we will have "in abundance" to share the overflow!!

> 3. <u>Drink Hag. 1 verse 6 c</u> "....*<u>you drink, but there is not enough to become drunk;</u>"*

My goodness, this is a profound word: we drink but not enough to become drunk!! Immediately the Lord referred me to the following scripture: *Eph 5:18*

And do not get drunk with wine, for that is dissipation, but be filled with the Spirit,

Being drunk in the natural, which the Lord abhors of course, is actually being "under the influence", in this instance, of a substance that if we have to much of it we lose our control over our body and soul in various degrees, depending on how much we drink. It is interesting how someone who in the natural sober state would be shy and timid yet after a couple of drinks become bold and loud!! They will pick a fight with someone who obviously would give them grief!! Peter the disciple became very bold "under the influence" (his spirit man) and preached the gospel boldly and without fear for his own life! *Act 4:8 Then Peter, filled with the Holy Spirit, said to them, "Rulers and elders of............"*

The Lord is referring to a spiritual drink. John the Baptist was filled with the Spirit from a very young age: *Luk 1:15 "For he will be great in the sight of the Lord, and he will drink no wine or liquor; and he will be filled with the Holy Spirit, while yet in his mother's womb.* Again the contrast to wine!

I believe the word drink in this passage refers to the Holy Spirit: *1Co 12:13 For by one Spirit we were all baptized into one body, whether Jews or Greeks, whether slaves or free, and we were all made to drink of one Spirit.*

This verse in Haggai therefore wants us to be not just filled with but to a point of "being drunk", under the influence! Boldness, humbleness, love for the Lord and our fellow man, wisdom and understanding the scriptures, etc. etc. to such an extent that : *Act 4:31 And when they had prayed, the place where they had gathered together was shaken, and they were all filled with the Holy Spirit, and began to speak the word of God with boldness.*

The Lord is actually telling us that we cannot labour without being filled to overflowing with Holy Spirit. I will explain in greater detail later in this book the extent and manner of being filled with the Spirit of God. Suffice it to say that Haggai received this word of "being drunk" in the Spirit as a lack in the body (Israel).

Too many critics in the church are condemning what is happening in some churches, labeling the work of the Holy Spirit as evil! I do not want to be in those who do so's shoes!! I know that some are emphasising aspects of the phenomenon and thus creating a wrong understanding of what the Lord wants to do. We are struggling to get past the flesh and its desire for fame and glory, rather serving the body and ministering in truth. However, we are to seek greater "infilling", to drink and drink UNTILL DRUNK!!

Joh 16:13 "But when He, the Spirit of truth, comes, He will guide you into all the truth; for He will not speak on His own initiative, but whatever He hears, He will speak; and He will disclose to you what is to come.

> 4. <u>Clothe: Hag. 1 verse 6 d</u> *"....ye clothe you, but there is none warm....;"*

The emphasis in this verse I believe is on the too little clothes which causes the lack of warmth. The very first thought that came to mind was Adam and Eve finding themselves naked and their own efforts to clothe themselves was futile. The Lord came and provided adequate clothing to keep them warm, to cover their nakedness.

Our spiritual clothing should protect us and be attractive to the unsaved, keeping us warm! Isaiah 52 verse 1 says:" *....put on thy strength, O Zion; put on thy beautiful garments, O Jerusalem...."*

<u>Gal 3:27</u> *For as many of you as have been baptized into Christ have put on Christ.*

<u>Eph 4:24</u> *And that ye put on the new man, which after God is created in righteousness and true holiness.* Our nakedness is removed when we are saved by the blood of the Lamb and we are again "clothed" by Him!!

In unity, clothed in righteousness and the Truth, much can be attained by the church. <u>Ecc 4:11</u> *Furthermore, if two lie down together they keep warm, but how can one be warm alone?* As a *church* we should be one as Jesus and the Father is one: *Joh 17:22 "And the glory which Thou hast given Me I have given to them; that they may be one, just as We are one; Joh 17:23 I in them, and Thou in Me, that they may be perfected in unity, that the world may know that Thou didst send Me, and didst love them, even as Thou didst love Me.*

Joh 14:12 "Truly, truly, I say to you, he who believes in Me, the works that I do shall he do also; and greater works than these shall he do; because I go to the Father. 13 "And whatever you ask in My name, that will I do, that the Father may be glorified in the Son. 14 "If you ask Me anything in My name, I will do it.

    5. <u>Wages: Hag. 1 verse 6 e</u> "*....and he who earns, earns wages to put into a purse with holes."*

In this verse I believe the purse with holes stands out as the crux of the message. It also implies that no mending is done and the holes remain. The spiritual meaning here is contained in this verse, amongst others: <u>Pro 10:16</u> *The wages of the righteous is life, The income of the wicked, punishment.* Our efforts are such that it could be of great value but our purse which must contain it has holes.

We see that the effect of the sin of Israel is visible in the land: Hag 1:10 "Therefore, because of you the sky has withheld its dew and the earth has withheld its produce. However, the Lord never leaves us devastated by our inability to rectify things as we will see later but suffice it to say that He calls us to just come back: Hag 1:12 .... And the people showed reverence for the LORD.

As soon as they admitted their lack, the Lord confirms His love and care for them: Hag 1:13 Then Haggai, the messenger of the LORD, spoke by the commission of the LORD to the people saying, " 'I am with you,' declares the LORD." The Lord then promises, because of their return to Him, to trust Him, Hag 2:9 'The latter glory of this house will be greater than the former,' says the LORD of hosts, 'and in this place I will give peace,' declares the LORD of hosts."

Chris Hamman

AS SWEET AS HONEY

Son_2:3 As the apple-tree among the trees of the wood, So is my beloved among the sons. I sat down under his shadow with great delight, And his fruit was sweet to my taste.

I (and I believe you as well) have found the word of God as sweet as honey many times, bringing hope through His promises to people as healing just as honey is to the physical body. Honey, raw honey, has many medicinal benefits. Raw honey, for instance, contains bee pollen, which is known to ward off infections, provide natural allergy relief and boost overall immunity. The processed type found on most shelves in shops lost much of its potency to do this. (John the Baptist must have consumed much raw honey which kept him in good health?). <u>It is the raw untainted (unprocessed) word of God</u> that will bring healing and restoration to the people, not a man made "processed" word of God. The only One who will ensure that God's word is undiluted and "unprocessed" is Holy Spirit. The following article from *Cheryl McGrath* in her "Bread for the Bride" is quoted with her permission, unaltered and fully in the paragraphs below as they completely underline what I believe God wants to convey here. God wants His "angels" to be His untainted voice, bringing heavenly sweetness that cleanses, to men:

He (John the Baptist) was said to prefer the isolated expanse of the wilderness to the noisy, populated villages and towns. People said he snacked on wild honey from the rock crevices and ate locusts for breakfast. And there were rumours an angel had announced his impending birth.

He must have been an imposing figure in his course camel hair tunic, his waist and thighs clad in leather, with his unkempt hair and beard only enhancing his wild appearance (Mat. 3:4). But most of all it was his eyes I suspect – eyes that fixed you and penetrated your soul before wandering away to a secret place known only to him. There was passion in those eyes. A dangerous, unworldly, irresistible passion that drew people, yet also alarmed them.

It had been hundreds of years since Israel had seen a prophet like this one. This John, who they called the Baptiser, reminded them of the ancient and renowned Elijah, who also covered himself in a hair tunic and leather girdle (2 Kings 1:8). Elijah had prayed for rain and the rain had come; Elijah had called down fire from heaven and slain 450 false prophets (1 Kings 18:40-45). Would John the Baptiser do similar wonders?

Israel wanted to know the answer. So Israel went out to see this strange new phenomenon for themselves.

"What did you go out to see?" Jesus would later ask the sign-seeking crowds. "A prophet?" (Matt. 11:9). Yes, they had gone to see a prophet, of course they had, for these were troubling times and a prophet's presence in Israel may mean God was about to deliver His people from the oppressive occupation of idol-worshiping Rome. After all, if Israel couldn't hope in God in these turbulent times, what else was there to hope in? But the one who Jesus would call "the burning and shining lamp" had not come to call fire down from heaven or slay idol-worshipers (John 5:35).

He had come as a witness and a revealer.

Investigators came from the religious authorities in Jerusalem to observe and examine this upstart 'prophet' who dared to invoke the esteemed Elijah. "Who are you?" they demanded. "The Messiah, Elijah, another Prophet?" No, none of those, was John's response. "Who then?" they insisted.

"I am the voice of one crying in the wilderness make straight the way of the Lord." (Jn. 1:19-23; Is. 40:3)

Oh, they knew those words from Isaiah well but would have been less than satisfied by the Baptiser's crafty answer. One claiming to be the Messiah or even Elijah they could bring to trial for blasphemy, but what do you do with a '**voice**'?

But the Baptiser had other things on his mind. He had been sent for a purpose and that purpose burned in his bones like hot coals. His time was short, and he knew it. So he told them: "There is One among you who you do not know who, coming after me, is preferred before me" (John. 1:26, 27). Or, in 21st century paraphrase: "I'm just the warm up act for Someone here you can't even see – if you think you've got problems with me you ain't seen nothing yet!"

And just one day after that rather testy conversation John the Baptiser, seeing Jesus nearby, declared to his disciples the reason he had been sent.

"Behold! The Lamb of God, who takes away the sin of the world. This is He of whom I said 'After me comes a Man who was preferred before me, for He was before me.' I did not know Him, **but that He should be revealed to Israel, therefore I came baptising with water**." (John. 1:29-31)

Though others may have been confused about it, John knew who he was. Up until the Holy Spirit revealed the Christ to him at the Jordan, John didn't even know the identity of Israel's coming Messiah (Jn. 1:32). But he knew who he was. And consequently he knew why he was here.

"But that He should be revealed to Israel...I came".

You and I, as members of the Bride of Christ, are currently in this world for a specific purpose. It is no co-incidence that we are alive here and now in this present chaotic age when hope is fading fast.

We are here as witness and revealer.

"You have sent to John, and he has borne witness to the truth", Jesus would say to His religious persecutors (John 5:33). John, *who lived and died under the Old Covenant, was indeed sent as Christ's witness, but was witness only to Christ coming in flesh and blood, not to His resurrection. We, the Bride-church of Christ, are the only living witness in this world that Christ is risen. That is the reason why Jesus said he who is least in the Kingdom is greater than John the Baptist (Mat. 11:11), for John died before the New Covenant was ratified.*

*The earliest church understood their identity as revealer and witness (Luke 24:28; Acts 1:8; 1:22; 2:32; 4:33; 5:32; 10:39; 13:31; 1 Jn. 5:10). Understand that you do not need to do anything to bear this same witness, for you have the witness in yourself (1 Jn. 5:10). This witness is not about house to house e evangelism, handing out tracts or preaching on street corners. If you are **in Christ**, then simply by **being** you are the living, breathing witness to His resurrection.*

*In the same way, each of us has a part to play in revealing Christ. Again, it is not about going to church, quoting scripture to your neighbour, or proving you're a nice person. If you are **in Christ** and genuinely keeping fellowship with Him, He can and will reveal Himself through you whenever and wherever He chooses to do so. John the Baptiser, the last Old Covenant prophet, was the 'lamp' but he was not the Light. But Jesus said His Bride would be the "light of the world" (Matt. 5:14).*

Imagine, then, the power and also the danger to enemies of the Cross that the combined presence of Christ's bridal company carries in this world.

My friends, we are a prophetic Bride. There is a deep abiding burning, a passion within each of us that defines who we are. It's time to get in touch with it.

*I am not talking about launching into ministry, getting busier at church or rushing off to some foreign mission field without the unction and direct sending of the Holy Spirit. I am talking about connecting with **Christ in us** to a depth we have not yet known. I am talking about learning to rest in Him so He can increase and* we can decrease. I am talking about walking in a level of communion with Him that lifts from us the burden to perform, and transforms us into His transparent, shining witnesses and revealers in this world. I am talking about knowing who we are and what our reason for being alive right now is. I am talking about not allowing the distractions of the daily news bulletins to define how we walk in this world.

The greatest enemy to that God-ordained prophetic passion in each of us is **not** Satan, the Defeated One. <u>It is man-ordained, man-controlled, man-organised religion.</u> The religious spirit can neither understand nor endure authentic Spirit-filled, Christ-centered passion. Man-controlled religion will always seek to rob us, violently at times, of whatever God-given passion burns within us. Man-controlled religion is happy to display a religious fervour that mimics the Holy Spirit, but true prophetic voices sent by God will always be a threat to false religion, because they will always call it for what it is – antichrist.

The sole reason the religious authorities came to interrogate John the Baptiser was to find a way to shut him down. The only way you can shut down a **voice** is silence it, and eventually that voice was silenced, but not before he fulfilled the purpose for which he was sent by God – to reveal Christ to Israel.

On this earth, John did not have access to the whole unfolding panorama that could be seen from Heaven's perspective. He was not God; he didn't know the end from the beginning. But he knew who he was and what he was here for, and that formed his perspective. And so can we.

To participate in God's unfolding purpose, we don't have to understand everything He's doing at the moment. We don't need to read every new book by the latest celebrity leaders, we don't have to attend all the coolest conferences, or own the most anointed worship CD's. We just need to understand who we are as Christ's corporate Bride and that our purpose for this hour is to reveal Christ – and then allow Him to fulfil that purpose through us *wherever He has placed us. He will take care of the bigger picture.*

Several years ago in a remote part of Kenya I was offered some fresh local honey. I imagined something similar to the honey available in western supermarkets. Instead I was presented with honeycomb straight form the hive, sweet and sticky, and still crawling with bees. It was pure wild honey – unrefined, undiluted, unfiltered.

Biblically, honey represents the sweetness of the pure Word of God while locusts symbolise destruction and invading armies (Ps. 19:7-10; Psalm 119:103; Sng. 4:11; Joel 1:4; Rev. 9:3, 7).

True prophets live in the wild abandon of pure and undiluted sweetness of communion with Christ, the living Word (honey). They also learn to walk with Him as overcomers in the midst of their spiritual enemies (locusts.) They become adept at both. But where is this Bride adorned in prophetic passion for the Bridegroom? Where are the fierce and penetrating voices of her prophets?

There are any number of voices that want to soothe our itching ears with a 'word' about our nation, our family or our ministry. There are countless websites that will attempt to explain exactly how current events fulfil biblical prophecy. There is no shortage of conferences that promise to boost us to 'a new level', make us into 'world changers', 'embrace, embolden and encourage us" and teach us to 'dive deep into ministry' or 'blaze with God's glory'*.

But where is the locust and honey eating prophetic Bride of Christ with the Wind in her hair and the Fire in her spirit that loves not her life and thunders the revelation of Christ to the world?

I choose to believe that she lives – within you, within me, within us.

I choose to believe that she is awakening.

I choose to believe we ain't seen nothing yet.

*These phrases are quoted from current Christian conference advertising.

© **Cheryl McGrath,** Bread for the Bride**, 2017. Copyright Notice: Permission is granted to freely reproduce any** Bread for the Bride **articles in emails or internet blogs, unaltered, and providing this copyright notice is included.**

Although this (above) word is for every Christian, I would like to state here that God is calling the "John the Baptists" amongst us leaders specifically as well. The call is to go deeper personally and to know that you and I are called to and will be blessed beyond what we ever could imagine, if we do. It will require walking in the dessert but the reward of heaven is immeasurable!!

Get the pure honey directly from source!! *Isa_55:1 "Ho! Everyone who thirsts, come to the waters; And you who have no money come, buy and eat. Come, buy wine and milk Without money and without cost.*

Chris Hamman

ADDRESSING ANGELS

Rev 2:1 Unto the angel of the church of Ephesus write; These things saith he that holdeth the seven stars in his right hand, who walketing in the midst of the seven golden candlesticks;

The core of this message is the fact that Revelation 2 and 3 is, I believe and was shown to me by the Lord, addressed to the spiritual leaders (Pastors, Preachers, Teachers, etc.) and not primarily to the congregations. (Please do not reject the word yet. Read on and accept the statement as is until more revelation is shared below. I believe you will be blessed beyond your imagination.) The implication that the congregation is involved is true but the letter addresses the spiritual leader (pastor prophet, etc.)!!! I will explain in more detail as you read on. (*To the angel of the church ....*) The purpose is for me to reveal what I "hear" the Lord is saying now to us spiritual leaders and explore what I see as His restorative work in the "last days". The (biblical) truth is always easy, simple and straightforward, not difficult and unclear.

If the department of education in South Africa would hear from outside sources that a particular school is not excelling in a particular area, the letter they prepare in this regard will not be addressed to the children at the school or the individual teacher but to the principal who should take action. Is this not how we should approach the letters to the seven churches recorded in Revelation? The one man (including woman) who must take action!!

For many years these chapters were basically ignored by us spiritual leaders due to all the various, sometimes conflicting interpretations by man! (O *servant of the Lord*, guard what has been entrusted to you, avoiding worldly *and* empty chatter *and* the opposing arguments of what is falsely called "knowledge"-)

My prayer is: *Lord, I realize the awesomeness and responsibility of speaking on Your behalf. I have prayed and asked that Holy Spirit direct my thoughts and mind in order to speak forth what Your heart desires for now. Like a child I come boldly and trust You as my Father and my God!*

This message is therefore humbly addressed to the pastor /preacher /prophet/teacher in leadership (responsible) in His church at large. Yes, this is an awesome truth, that the letters recorded in Revelation 2 and 3 are addressed to the "chosen" spiritual leaders and even though it includes the "church members", the fact is only the leader can initiate change or correction of a particular church. I will try to explain this in greater detail below as the message is so awesome, so clear and dramatic that you will have to ask the Lord if what I am sharing is all the truth, is there more and is it for now.

The message I received from the Lord is that actually His (stars) pastors, teachers, prophets and priests in leadership must listen and take action. Every symbol used in Revelation 1, 2 and 3 was, I believe, especially and carefully chosen by the Lord to convey His holy will and desire for the church, the Bride of Christ through His angels/stars. If you are a member of a church reading this and feel it needs to be heard by your own spiritual leader, please pass it on. If you feel you just want to pray this for your congregation, please do so.

I also want to admit that I see myself as a "minister" and therefore this message includes me. This is actually a love letter as you will see in reading on. These letters (Rev. 2 and 3) and Rev. Chapter 1, place spiritual leaders very close to the Lord. They are like "angels" to Him. My dear, dear brother in Christ, I would desire that you and I hear the heart of God and that our love for Him will increase dramatically and our willingness to obey become an obsession of our very being!!

The next chapter deals with the fact that the leaders in the church are to be "in His hand" so to speak. They are sent by Him, used by Him, become His voice, His heart, His glory on earth.

GRIPPED BY THE LORD

Rev 1:16 And he had in his right hand seven stars: and out of his mouth went a sharp two edged sword: and his countenance *was* as the sun shineth in his strength.

The most beautiful words of Jesus to those He called to be shepherds of His people is this profound address: *"to the angel..."*!!

In other Bible translations the word: messenger" is used. He calls them "angels". We will discuss this in more detail later but I want to emphasise here that He clearly has a special place in His heart for His shepherds on earth!! In the same chapter of Revelation He calls them "stars". This too will be discussed later in more detail. Suffice it to say here that I am under the unction of the Holy Spirit to deliver a message, which I do not feel worthy (to be chosen) to be the messenger of. It is a message that contains the call of the Lord to His called ones in ministry to renew their relationship with Him as His "angels" and "stars"!!

I believe all who minister are "shepherds" and therefore are included in this message. Prophet or evangelist or teacher, or spiritual leader, please, you are included.

In Rev 1 verse 16 we can imagine what John sees, Jesus our Lord standing with 7 stars (gripped) in His right hand. These stars represent the 7 angels and the 7 angels are the leadership of the churches mentioned (Rev 1 verse 20).

I have been given these four aspects that I feel need to be carefully considered here, i.e.:
1. Angels,
2. Stars,
3. Our Lord holding them and
4. In His right hand!

Angels

An awesome statement and revelation in verse 20 of chapter 1 is that the Lord is holding 7 stars (angels) in His right hand. These stars are the **angels** of the churches as our Lord explains in verse 20. Some argue that these may be angels assigned to the churches but that is a misinterpretation. The Lord will not have John, a mortal, write a letter to an angel. He gives them direct orders in heaven. Nowhere in Scripture is there any incident where someone of earthly nature instructed an angel. They are ministers and messengers directly from God our Father! Furthermore angels do not sin (if they do they are cast out), especially not the sins mentioned here! Furthermore the Lord is saying that if his "angel" do not listen, He will remove the church (lampstand – chapter 1 verse 20) from that pastor/leader, etc. (Rev 2 verse 5) No angel has a church under its control or leadership! No angel is responsible for human sins!! The truth is far more awesome and amasing!

Why would the Lord use the term angel here when all the rest of Scripture actually mean heavenly beings!!   I gave this some thought and after meditating a bit the following is revealed to me:

The use of the term "angel" is very prophetic and specific. .Angels are not just messengers. In Hebrew, an "angel" is called malakh (מַלְאָךְ), a word that basically means "messenger" or representative (from the root לאך, meaning "to send"). As we see in scripture they minister, execute power, wield swords, touch men, appear in dreams, are physically seen and experienced, know exactly what God wants to do, speak as God (messengers) and they guide or

The term "minister" would seem to fit them more comfortably than the term messenger. They even ministered to Jesus before His crucifixion. Jesus in His human body experienced extreme anguish for what lay ahead and God sent an angel to minister to Him! This then gives us a better understanding of why the Lord uses the term "angel" for His earthly ministers!

The term messenger used in some translations is therefore unfortunate and provides a limited image of the full truth. Angels are constantly in the Lords presence, worship Him and knows exactly what He wants, His will and His plans. They live in heaven where time, distance and space has no barriers or limitations. They are constantly in the glory of the Lord! They are sent by Him and this fact gave me the impression that God is saying that the ministers on earth are His sent ones!

It is therefore clear in my mind that:

Ministers should get their message directly from the Lord, not second hand.
They are sent ones by the Lord Himself, not by a synod or other person or body!
They proclaim the word of God and establish a godly standard.
They minister to the flock.
They serve the body.
They are (to be) "in the presence" of the Most Holy One constantly!
The following scripture underlines this awesome truth: *Mal 2:7 "For the lips of a priest should preserve knowledge, and men should seek instruction from his mouth; for he is the messenger of the LORD of hosts.*

The Lord led me to read "The Miracle of the Scarlet Thread" written by Richard Booker (again) where he deftly deals with the connection of the Old Testament or old covenant and the new covenant. We need to fully understand what God has done through the cross and the Lamb of God, His Son! He cut covenant with everyone who believes in Jesus, thereby He, as part of this covenant, gave us His "sword" His "clothes" and His everything.....the Holy Spirit, even His power and His love! I believe the measure of these is increased to His ministers. We read that Paul did more miracles than the average apostle.

Angels have great authority given by the Lord. They have great power to execute the will of the Lord. In one instance the Lord tells an angel to withdraw his hand of destruction as He has decided not to destroy anymore!! You and I too have authority for example, to cast out demons like Jezebel but because we do not, the Lord warns!! Jezebel is a controlling spirit and often works through women although men are also susceptible to this spirit. Some wives or a specific female member are controlling the pastor by manipulation and the pastor knows he is being manipulated. God is angry that we tolerate this spirit of manipulation.

No one has seen God (except for Moses) and live to tell the tale! So no angel described in the Old Testament is God. That interpretation is unfortunately misplaced. God never appears as an angel. He appears to Moses whilst shielding him in a rock cleft and allows Abraham to see His "back". He sends an Angel to minister to Jesus. The disciples saw the angel and wrote about it. Nor is Jesus one of the angels described in most of the writings. However, He may have appeared thus to some but it cannot be irrefutably proven through scripture. Angels represent the Lord and act for Him and as Him! You and I, in ministry must realise we to are representing God, representing Jesus. You and I are sent by Him! Much of what the Lord promised would happen in ministry is attributed to the leader or minister of the Gospel. The more time spent in His presence the more we will shine forth and represent Him in truth.

I want to make it clear here that the Lord Himself appoints. Paul did not appoint Timothy but Paul recognised the calling and the "sent" one! Bodies created, for example synods, are to take note and not appoint!! Once a human body appoints, the appointee is under their control. This should never be!! I know this is a controversial subject but the truth is the truth. 1Ti 1:18 *This command I entrust to you, Timothy, my son, <u>in accordance with the prophecies previously made concerning you,</u> that by them you may fight the good fight,* It is the acknowledgment that God is sending someone that needs to be accepted and supported. Your boss is God! No one else. Your covering is God, no one else. All that is required is to ensure we are surrounded by godly men and women to be our sounding boards on occasion. Only when we are totally dependent on God will we be able to hear Him clearly.

Using the word "angel" the Lord, I believe, underlines a major spiritual position and an office or calling. Also very significant is that angels "come from heaven" and "from the presence of the Lord" What I believe the Lord is actually saying and really "conveying", is that His pastors, preachers, reverends, are as angels to Him.

They are sent by Him (appointed), they represent the One who is in the midst of the seven lampstands, they minister on His behalf and they serve the church (lampstand) for Him. They are aware of heaven in its fullness having spent time with the Lord Himself.

(Paul writes: **Ti 1:1** *Paul, an apostle of Jesus Christ <u>by the commandment of God our Saviour</u>, and Lord Jesus Christ, which is our hope;* and in *2Ti 1:1 Paul, an apostle of Jesus Christ <u>by the will of God</u>, according to the promise of life which is in Christ Jesus,*)

If you put your name in place of Paul and if you are a pastor place you're calling in the place of apostle it would read thus:

<u>Dave</u>, a <u>pastor</u> of Jesus Christ by the commandment of God our Saviour, and Lord Jesus Christ, which is our hope; or.......
<u>Andrew</u>, a <u>prophet</u> of Jesus Christ by the will of God, according to the promise of life which is in Christ Jesus.......

To the Galatians he (Paul) writes: Gal 1 v 1: *Paul, an apostle, (not of men, neither by man, but by Jesus Christ, and God the Father, who raised him from the dead ;)*

Now my dear brother, place your name here and see what happens: Andrew, a pastor, (not of men, neither by man, but by Jesus Christ, and God the Father, who raised me from the dead ;)…….

Please pause a moment when placing your name and calling in these verses and ponder the significance thereof. Please do not rush on but consider the awesomeness of this!! Pray that the Lord will allow this truth to sink in to your heart!

1Ti 4:6 *If thou put the brethren in remembrance of these things, thou shalt be **a good minister of Jesus Christ**, nourished up in the words of faith and of good doctrine, whereunto thou hast attained.* Note here again the terminology used: "minister of Jesus Christ". I believe ministers have forgotten that they are His ministers, His sent ones, in Revelation referred to as "angels"!!!!

What is important too, is that he wants His pastors, etc. to be in His presence as the angels are!! They must be so committed to the Lord that they shine like angels do!!!

(Stephen: *Act_6:15 And fixing their gaze on him, all who were sitting in the Council saw his face like the face of an angel.*)

Stars

Mat 5:14 *"You are the light of the world. A city set on a hill cannot be hidden.*
"Nor do men light a lamp, and put it under the peck-measure, but on the lampstand; and it gives light to all who are in the house. Let your light shine before men in such a way that they may see your good works, and glorify your Father who is in heaven".

Stars do not need the sun as planets do. They have their own light. No star reflects another star's light. (1 Co 15:41) What comes to mind here is the following. God created the stars to also distinguish between darkness and light, and that individually!! Each one hears directly from the Lord, not from each other or from man!! Stars differ in size, intensity and form. They find themselves having light!! They do not reflect light. This implies that God has His ministers or spiritual leaders in His hand to do His will. He equipped them individually. They differ in intensity, size and form. We must never compare ourselves with another ministry or saint. We are to shine forth with what we are given.

Gen 1:16 And *God made two great lights; the greater light to rule the day, and the lesser light to rule the night: he made the stars also. 17 And God set them in the firmament of the heaven to give light upon the earth, 18 And to rule over the day and over the night, and to divide the light from the darkness:* You may say these words refer to the physical creation and indeed they do. However, as so many places in scripture there is a hidden spiritual truth. You and I are responsible to rule over darkness (sin, sickness, inner conflicts, etc.) You have a special anointing. Gripped by the Lord. Rule over darkness in the church and in our own lives.

I believe the Lord is saying (In Revelation 1) His chosen pastor/preacher/teacher must shine in the church…light overcomes darkness, in fact it brings order in chaos. He or she must shine which may indicate they are in the presence of the Lord. They were sent to bring division between light and darkness. They must ensure darkness does not have dominion in their own lives and the church they serve by ruling over it (darkness) in the spirit. (Rom 1 v 9: Paul says "…whom I serve in the spirit….").

I will share more about the Holy Spirit later. He is a most holy personality!! (1Th 4:8 He *therefore that despiseth, despiseth not man, but God, who hath also given unto us His Holy Spirit.*)

Holding them

Our Lord has these stars under His authority and control. They are His! It is His possession, they belong to Him. He created them to shine and "rule" in His church. Not over men but over darkness!! As long as He has them in His hand He can "use" them effectively. Remember that they are likened to angels and angels, just like Satan, may choose! As long as they stay willingly in His hand, He can use them with His right hand….. Having them in His hand and standing between the Lampstands (churches) we may derive that The Lord Himself ministers to His Bride through the stars in His hand, the angels or ministers / spiritual leaders of the churches.

The word "hand" in Hebrew is "yad" and sometimes translated as "influence" (see Daniel 8 verse 25). We could say the stars are under the Lord's "influence". One Webster's dictionary defines "influence" as *the power or capacity of causing an effect in indirect or tangible ways.* The fact is that the Lord never demands or forces anyone to do His will, therefore being under His "influence" (willingly) would seem a proper explanation?

Please feel comfortable in the thought that you are in His hand, gripped or held by Him. It denotes both responsibility and comfort.

Right hand

It seems from Scripture that the Lord's right hand is the one He uses to act with specifically (like a right handed person in the flesh) The following verses confirm this:

Gen 48 v 14 to 18; Exod 15 v 6 and 8; Lev. 14 v 14; Job 40 v 14 and Ps 16 v 11. Here are some verses that further confirm this:

Psa 16:11 Thou wilt make known to me the path of life; In Thy presence is fullness of joy; In Thy right hand there are pleasures forever.

Psa_18:35 Thou hast also given me the shield of Thy salvation, And Thy right hand upholds me; And Thy gentleness makes me great.
Psa_21:8 Your hand will find out all your enemies; Your right hand will find out those who hate you.
Psa_48:10 As is Thy name, O God, So is Thy praise to the ends of the earth; Thy right hand is full of righteousness.

You and I, as spiritual leader of His church are in the Lord's right hand to accomplish what He wants to do. Not your own ways, His ways.!!! To stay in His hand therefore requires of us to follow His ways and it is clear that the Lord will not deviate from the pattern He has set. "My house shall be a house of prayer"!!! You shall **love** the Lord your God with all your strength, with all your soul and with all your mind.

Chris Hamman

A PRAYING BRIDE

The Lord has provided a very special love, gifting, grace and mercy to these called ones and therefore expects much from them in terms of nurturing the flock and expanding His kingdom on earth. To His apostles He commanded:

Mat 28:19 "Go therefore and make disciples of all the nations, baptizing them in the name of the Father and the Son and the Holy Spirit, 20 teaching them to observe all that I commanded you; and lo, I am with you always, even to the end of the age." Do we realise this word refers to the pastor, evangelist, preacher, etc.? Not all of us will baptise people will we?

To Timothy Paul writes:
1Ti 6:13 I charge you in the presence of God, who gives life to all things, and of Christ Jesus, who testified the good confession before Pontius Pilate, that you keep the commandment without stain or reproach until the appearing of our Lord Jesus Christ, which He will bring about at the proper time--He who is the blessed and only Sovereign, the King of kings and Lord of lords;

In Revelation 2 and 3 a warning is sounded where the "angels" (shepherds) are found wanting and this is why I have to bring this message today! ....*that we keep the commandment without stain or reproach……*

As we see the hour coming closer and the coming of our Lord eminent, shepherds should be on their knees for themselves, the children of God and the lost, basically as a perpetual event where hearts and minds are set on Him until .... until ......He comes!!

Isa_56:7 Even those I will bring to My holy mountain, And make them joyful in My house of prayer. Their burnt offerings and their sacrifices will be acceptable on My altar; For My house will be called <u>a house of prayer for all the peoples.</u>"

Mat_21:13 And He *said to them, "It is written, 'MY HOUSE SHALL BE CALLED A HOUSE OF PRAYER'; but you are making it a ROBBERS' DEN."

The Jews are today in the year 2018 (re-) building the (3rd) temple, creating the various vessels and the altar of sacrifice, training their sons as Levites to serve in the temple and are seeking a red unblemished heifer for the sacrifice as predicted in the Book of Daniel!:

Dan 8:17 So he came near to where I was standing, and when he came I was frightened and fell on my face; but he said to me, "Son of man, understand that the vision <u>pertains to the time of the end</u>."

Dan 12:11 "And from the time that <u>the regular sacrifice</u> is abolished, and the abomination of desolation is set up, there will be 1,290 days.

2Th 2:4 who opposes and exalts himself above every so-called god or object of worship, so that he takes his seat in the temple of God, displaying himself as being God.

So it is clear there will be a time when Israel will again follow the sacrificial laws of Moses and this eventually destroyed by a foreign king who *"exalts himself above every so-called god or object of worship"*.

The fact that these prophecies and others that are being fulfilled in our day gives rise to us reminding ourselves of warnings that are crucial in the last days, such as:

Mat 25:8 "And the foolish (Virgins) said to the prudent, 'Give us some of your oil, for our lamps are going out.' 9 "But the prudent answered, saying, 'No, there will not be enough for us and you too; go instead to the dealers and buy some for yourselves.' 10 "And while they were going away to make the purchase, the bridegroom came, and those who were ready went in with him to the wedding feast; **and the door was shut.**

I believe that some of us have become more enamoured by the people, who esteem us, the organisation (church) and the building and maintenance of a congregation than the spiritual condition of the individuals within and a true love for the Bridegroom. Events and their success became a distracting issue as they (the events) tend to rob people of their time and energy. The truth that without Holy Spirit it is impossible, totally impossible, to live the life required from us as Christians, have been lost or never addressed! The American pastor Rick Joiner puts it this way in his book "A Message to the Glorious Church":

*The apostolic mandate was not to build churches or ministries but to labour until Christ was formed in His people. (*Gal *4:19 My little children, of whom I travail in birth again until Christ be formed in you,)*

He furthermore stated that Ephesus means "Full Purpose" and it is no coincidence that the first letter in Revelation 2 is addressed to the "Angel" of the Christians in Ephesus! Lack of first love is mentioned first!! Our goal is to love from a pure heart, a good conscience and a sincere faith (1 Tim 1 v 5). We need to attain to our full purpose, all of us.

In 2Pe 1:4 we read "Whereby are given unto us exceeding great and precious promises: that by these ye might be **partakers of the**

divine nature*, having escaped the corruption that is in the world through lust.*

Each individual Christian should be a partaker of the divine nature (Of Jesus)! He who lacks this is blind: *2Pe 1:9 But he that lacketh these things is blind, and cannot see afar off, and hath forgotten that he was purged from his old sins.*

Are we concerned for this to be the goal of each of the sheep in our fold? Are we on our knees for this to manifest amongst our people? What is the true condition of the congregation, measured against the requirements of our love and faith? I have experienced much fleshly love but see very little agape love abound amongst us!!

Jesus didn't say that all men would know we are His disciples by our doctrine, our rituals, our hatred for sin, or even by the way we express our love for God. He said very clearly, that the one characteristic that would cause the world to identify us as His followers, **is our love, one for another.**

This same night, the Lord prayed to His Father using this same thought saying, *"That they all may be one; as thou, Father, art in Me, and I in Thee, that they also may be one in Us: that the world may believe that Thou hast sent Me" (Jn. 17:21)*. The only way that Christ's body will be one as the Father and Jesus are One, is through God's kind of love.

Unity of believers that can only come through a genuine God-kind of love is the greatest tool for evangelism that the church has or will ever have, according to Jesus. The early church didn't have the massive organizational structures that we see today or the ability to travel anywhere in the world in just a matter of hours. They certainly did not come close to spending as much money, in proportion to us, to spread the gospel. And yet, the pagans of Thessalonica said of Paul and his companions, "These that have turned the world upside down are come hither also" (Acts 17:6).

They had evangelized the known world in less than thirty years (A Message to the Glorious Church - Rick Joiner).

We who are to be the heart and mind of God, His "angels" are told we have not fulfilled all the Lord required from us. Jesus Christ writes to us specifically and states, "This I have against you...."!!!! Not our congregation, not the organisation, but us!! This message as contained in this book and its aim is for us to perhaps seek forgiveness by repentance and to obey the Lord. "Repent therefore unless I come and remove your lampstand"!!! The church must arise to its full potential and it has to begin with His "angels".

I hear the Lord calling again and His mercy abounds once more...so today if you hear His voice do not delay!! The most awesome truth about our utterly merciful God is reflected in the words of the prophet Hosea when he writes: Hos 11:8 *How can I give you up, O Ephraim? How can I surrender you, O Israel? How can I make you like Admah? How can I treat you like Zeboiim? My heart is turned over within Me, All My compassions are kindled. 9 I will not execute My fierce anger; I will not destroy Ephraim again. For I am God and not man, the Holy One in your midst, And I will not come in wrath.*

Our condition is due to a lack of knowledge, in many cases, rejected knowledge. We believe and are comfortable with our feelings and what our human intellect can contain: *Hos 4:6 My people are destroyed for lack of knowledge. Because you have rejected knowledge, I also will reject you from being My priest. Since you have forgotten the law of your God, I also will forget your children.* He also stated through this prophet that: *Hos 4:1 Listen to the word of the LORD, O sons of Israel, For the LORD has a case against the inhabitants of the land, Because there is no faithfulness or kindness Or knowledge of God in the land.*

Hos 4:2 There is swearing, deception, murder, stealing, and adultery. They employ violence, so that bloodshed follows bloodshed.

Hos 4:3 Therefore the land mourns, And everyone who lives in it languishes Along with the beasts of the field and the birds of the sky; And also the fish of the sea disappear.

As we can see this is amongst His own people and He says *"My heart is turned over within Me"* God is in anguish and it is us, our fault!!! We grieve Him daily!! He loves us yet we keep on sinning!!

Shepherd, if you think this is not you or your congregation, think again. God says even the fish and the beasts of the field are suffering today due to his children not listening!!! (....*Along with the beasts of the field and the birds of the sky; And also the fish of the sea disappear).*

Before we can ever fulfil the great commission of Matthew 28:19-20, there must be an urgent desire for revival and of love in the church, where doctrine and ritual take a "back seat", so that we really, passionately love one another. We can no longer delay and ignore the call!! **The most powerful weapon the Lord gave us, I believe, is prayer. Pray always and in all circumstances and conditions.** *Mat_14:23 And when he had sent the multitudes away, he went up into a mountain apart to pray: and when the evening was come, he was there alone. 1Th_5:17 Pray without ceasing. Luk_6:12 And it came to pass in those days, that he went out into a mountain to pray, and continued all night in prayer to God.* **Jesus Himself praying all night!** *He is our example is He not?*

Praying for revival for ourselves and the saints require a sacrifice of time, much time and perseverance with faith that He promised: *Mar_11:24 Therefore I say unto you, What things so ever ye desire, when ye pray, believe that ye receive them, and ye shall have them.*

CLOTHING THE BRIDE

Hos 2:1 – 3: Say ye unto your brethren, Ammi; and to your sisters, Ruhamah.
Plead with your mother, plead: for she is not my wife, neither am I her husband: let her therefore put away her whoredoms out of her sight, and her adulteries from between her breasts; Lest I strip her naked, and set her as in the day that she was born, and make her as a wilderness, and set her like a dry land, and slay her with thirst.

A church that is not following the Master is described as an adulterer, a whore, bringing forth children that is not acceptable to the Lord. The Lord says "plead with her, to turn back, to return as a bride!

In verse 17 of Song of Solomon chapter 2 we read *"Turn, My beloved, and be thou like a roe or a young hart upon the mountain of Bether". The meaning of Bether is "separation". This was at a point where the bride was seeking the Bridegroom but had not found Him. Now, in Chapter 8 verse 14, Bether is not mentioned but rather the "mountain of spices". The Church has passed through seasons of lapse and separation when intimate fellowship with her Lord was all but lost. Let it be the sincere intention of His bride* (in these last days of nearness to His coming), *that she may meet Him in the mountain of spices...<u>in the sweet fragrance of a renewed first love and the white fire of true devotion to Him alone</u>...* (Taken from "Make Haste My Beloved"- Frances Roberts).

When Jesus cleared the temple of the money changers and sellers of goods, His alarm (frowning face?) was for the lack of love and reverence for His Father and the people of the Lord. These men were just in it for enriching themselves at the cost of poor people and those who came to worship. His eyes must have portrayed an anger not often seen in Him!! In Revelation 1 John the disciple sees Him again now with those burning eyes. He could have been reminded of the zeal of the Lord? (Rev 1:14 *And His head and His hair were white like white wool, like snow; and His eyes were like a flame of fire ;*) However, I believe that this time Jesus showed a determination and a seriousness of purpose rather than anger. His words reveals His absolute determination, what it is He requires, who He is talking to and why: Rev 2:1 *"To the angel of the church in Ephesus write...*

The Lord who sits at the right hand of God, the Lord to whom all things have been given, both in heaven and on earth, is speaking to His sent ones, the angels in His right hand. This is at the heart of this message (to the shepherds of the Lord His "stars" and "angels" (Rev. 1 and 2). The One who has His stars in His hand, His "angels")

This message is a call for many "angels" to return to His right hand and *do His complete will.* that is, before wrong influences gave rise to compromising prayer-time, compromising a love relationship, giving rise to wrong choices and decisions, wrong motivations, which again resulted in weak teachings and preaching. Above all the lack of true love for Him!! He promised in so many scriptures that He will be the Teacher, yet the teachings of man prevail and the judgement of men is followed. God's Word can only be interpreted by the Spirit of the Lord yet man's interpretations are followed and taught! Ps 127 verse 1 states: *Unless the Lord builds the house, they labour in vain who built it.* In the Lord's prayer we hear: Mat 6:10 'Thy *kingdom come. Thy will be done, On earth as it is in heaven.*

Are we building the church, clothing the bride, as He commanded, by following His will, His design, or are we building as we see fit?

The scary part of our falling away is that we are doing some things right (Some preaching and teaching is right): Rev 2:6 *'Yet this you do have, that you hate the deeds of the Nicolaitans, which I also hate.* Rev 2:13 *'I know where you dwell, where Satan's throne is; and you hold fast My name, and did not deny My faith, even in the days of Antipas, My witness, My faithful one, who was killed among you, where Satan dwells.* Rev 2:19 *'I know your deeds, and your love and faith and service and perseverance, and that your deeds of late are greater than at first.*

We may be deceived in that we are doing things we think are correct (even a sort of love that we feel is acceptable to Him) and biblical but we are not hearing Him, we have ignored Him. Revelation 2 and 3 is a clear case of this fact. The "angels" of these churches are not doing all God's will and that is what He requires from us...all His will.

Look at these verses:

Eph 4:11 *And He gave some as apostles, and some as prophets, and some as evangelists, and some as pastors and teachers, 12 for the equipping of the saints for the work of service, to the building up of the body of Christ; 13 until we all attain to the unity of the faith, and of the knowledge of the Son of God, to a mature man, to the measure of the stature which belongs to the fullness of Christ.*

He gave these ministries to the church to equip and form all to the image of Jesus Christ!!

1Co 12:28 *And God has appointed in the church, first apostles, second prophets, third teachers, then miracles, then gifts of healings, helps, administrations, various kinds of tongues. 29 All are not apostles, are they? All are not prophets, are they? All are not teachers, are they? All are not workers of miracles, are they?* 1Co 12:30 *All do not have gifts of healings, do they? All do not speak with tongues, do they? All do not interpret, do they?*

God has appointed? God has appointed?? What have we done with this will of the Lord, that there should be these ministries in the church?

Mar 16:15 And *He said to them, "Go into all the world and preach the gospel to all creation. 16 "He who has believed and has been baptized shall be saved; but he who has disbelieved shall be condemned. 17 "And these signs will accompany those who have believed: in My name <u>they will cast out demons, they will speak with new tongues; 18 they will pick up serpents, and if they drink any deadly poison, it shall not hurt them; they will lay hands on the sick, and they will recover."*

Do we not understand and can we not discern: Do we not understand that where God moves the enemy countermoves? He will falsify each manifestation so that we will reject it all as false, not enquiring of the Lord but ourselves condemning what the Holy Spirit wants to do in our midst?.

Gal 3:1 O *foolish Galatians, who hath bewitched you, that ye should not obey the truth, before whose eyes Jesus Christ hath been evidently set forth, crucified among you? : 2 This only would I learn of you, Received ye the Spirit by the works of the law, or by the hearing of faith? : 3 Are ye so foolish? having begun in the Spirit, are ye now made perfect by the flesh?*

By preaching and teaching without the Holy Spirit there will be no change and no lasting fruit. The evidence should be there for all to see and experience!! Love amongst each other, Godly love, agape love is one sure evidence? Loving Him first will result in such evidence amongst us. All else will flow from this love, powerful love!!

I have heard preachers pray that the Holy Spirit have His way but there is just no evidence! Nothing happens but one man speaking and teaching then tea and coffee then home, next up is the prayer team, etc. Something is dramatically wrong and I mean dramatically!!! Hugs and how are you's aplenty but it is superficial most times.

What God is saying to us, we comfortably pass on to someone else but we do not do ourselves? Due to lack of understanding we grieve Him!!! God's people need healing and knowledge. They need the Holy Spirit of Truth!! The one requirement for the gifts to operate godly is the presence of godly love.

What about these commands from the Lord:

Isa 56:7 Even those I will bring to My holy mountain, And make them joyful in My house of prayer. Their burnt offerings and their sacrifices will be acceptable on My altar; For My house will be called a house of prayer for all the peoples."

Mat 21:13 And He *said to them, "It is written, 'MY HOUSE SHALL BE CALLED A HOUSE OF PRAYER'; but you are making it a ROBBERS' DEN."

Mar 11:17 And He *began* to teach and say to them, "Is it not written, 'MY HOUSE SHALL BE CALLED A HOUSE OF PRAYER FOR ALL THE NATIONS'? But you have made it a ROBBERS' DEN."

I am convinced that the church or congregation should be doing corporately what each and every Christian should be doing individually, that is, to worship the Lord in Spirit and in truth (John 4 verse 24). By the impartation and encouragement of Holy Spirit our experience should include times where the glory of the Lord descends as at Pentecost and during the inauguration of the first temple built by Solomon, the king. Spirit filled people experiencing and radiating joy and love should be the hallmark of any church! It is impossible for anyone to worship God without the impartation of Holy Spirit. It is the operation of Holy Spirit within us that enables us to worship God acceptably through the Person Jesus the Christ, who is Himself God. During the Welsh revival people queued at police stations, repenting of their sins, not knowing where else to go! We really really need Holy Spirit to come and cleanse us, convince us of our sins and to help us to persevere in prayer until He comes.

The Lord God seeks from all of us a type of worship that is acceptable to Him and I believe He is calling His Pastors, Preachers, Evangelists, Prophets, Teachers, etc. to accomplish this in the congregations. There is just too much violence, rape and corruption in the world. Because the church is silent it becomes ineffective. Lack of love, caring and godly principles amongst us is unacceptable as is the jezebel spirit Revelations is referring to. Yet in Hosea we read: *Hos 2:14 Therefore, behold, I will allure her, and bring her into the wilderness, and speak comfortably unto her.*

Hos 2:17 For I will take away the names of Baalim out of her mouth, and they shall no more be remembered by their name. And in that day will I make a covenant for them with the beasts of the field, and with the fowls of heaven, and with the creeping things of the ground: and I will break the bow and the sword and the battle out of the earth, and will make them to lie down safely And I will betroth thee unto me for ever; yea, I will betroth thee unto me in righteousness, and in judgment, and in lovingkindness, and in mercies. I will even betroth thee unto me in faithfulness: and thou shalt know the

LORD. And it shall come to pass in that day, I will hear, saith the LORD, I will hear the heavens, and they shall hear the earth; And the earth shall hear the corn, and the wine, and the oil; and they shall hear Jezreel. And I will sow her unto me in the earth; and I will have mercy upon her that had not obtained mercy; and I will say to them which were not my people, Thou art my people; and they shall say, Thou art my God.

When the prophets of old were instructed to speak by our God they were expected to not consider their own safety, but to speak. They were ignored, stoned and killed by the dozens by the ruling kings. Their words were not popular nor was it acceptable to them (the rulers). The following revelations may well cause many to have me "stoned" but I have to bring it as received. However, as in all scripture, our merciful Father asks us to turn, He is calling by the very word we feel condemns us or reprimands us.

Sharing what I have heard from the Lord involves me as well so I cannot distance myself from what I believe He is saying to the church today. I also realize that His word may be mixed with my imperfect understanding or my ear that needs to hear.

I have found it very difficult to share this word as my own flesh rebelled against this word many times, or at the least was very uncomfortable and I even felt guilty (I have been forgiven) as the message became more and more clear.

Revelations came as I wrote and many times I rewrote passages due to greater understanding and appropriate scriptures supporting issues I felt uncomfortable with in the beginning. My own lack became more and more evident and I am on my knees for it. So here it is in your hand to read.

Please note that where I refer to church it includes our Jewish brothers, in fact because of them we are included (see Annexure C).

Chris Hamman

THE BEAUTIFUL BRIDE

Joh_3:29 *"He who has the bride is the bridegroom; but the friend of the bridegroom, who stands and hears him, rejoices greatly because of the bridegroom's voice. And so this joy of mine has been made full.*

Mat_22:37 and *He said to him, "'you shall **love** the Lord your God with all your heart, and with all your soul, and with all your mind.'*

Dear reader, please be patient as you read the following chapter dealing with love, the love between the Bridegroom and the bride. It is absolutely essential that we not only understand but that we develop a love for the Lord that we may not have experienced before. That we go deeper and deeper. The Lord Himself brought me to what I am to share with you.

Son 1:3 *"Your oils have a pleasing fragrance, Your name is like purified oil; Therefore the maidens love you. Draw me after you and let us run together! The king has brought me into his chambers." "We will rejoice in you and be glad; We will extol your **love** more than wine. Rightly do they love **you**."*

A 92 years old retired pastor's own witness, downloaded from Christian Breaking News (19 October 2016) in connection with agape love is so appropriate, and I quote:

While watching a little TV on Sunday instead of going to church, I watched a Church in Atlanta honoring one of its senior pastors who had been retired many years. He was 92 at that time and I wondered why the Church even bothered to ask the old gentleman to preach at that age.

After a warm welcome, introduction of this speaker, and as the applause quieted down he rose from his high back chair and walked slowly, with great effort and a sliding gate to the podium. Without a note or written paper of any kind he placed both hands on the pulpit to steady himself and then quietly and slowly he began to speak..

"When I was asked to come here today and talk to you, your pastor asked me to tell you what was the greatest lesson ever learned in my 50 odd years of preaching. I thought about it for a few days and boiled it down to just one thing that made the most difference in my life and sustained me through all my trials.

The one thing that I could always rely on when tears and heart break and pain and fear and sorrow paralyzed me... The only thing that would comfort was this verse...

> *"Jesus loves me this I know.*
> *For the Bible tells me so.*
> *Little ones to Him belong,*
> *We are weak but He is strong.*
> *Yes, Jesus loves me...*
> *The Bible tells me so."*

In Joh 3 verse 16 we read that God loved us so much that He gave His only Son to redeem us, to save us, to bring us back to Him. I am asking myself, do we really understand this love? Abraham was tested and in obedience he took his only heir to his inheritance, the one who would carry his name to the next generation, the one he thought would become a mighty nation as God promised, and prepared to sacrifice him. God then provided a substitute and Isaac was spared. This act actually portrays what we deserve as sinners. But God, But God, in His utter mercy and love has planned to provide a better substitute than an animal.

When Jesus the Christ hung on the cross, God did not seek a substitute. He turned His face away when Jesus died, Who, paying the price in obedience and in love for the people God would give

Him, His own "body". He was beaten to an unrecognisable (dis)human being. God just could not face this sacrifice, His Son on the cross!! What sort of love is this? How could He give His only Son for us as a sacrifice!! Thousands upon thousands of animal sacrifices were offered in anticipation of this final sacrifice, Jesus the unblemished, sinless sacrifice, to pay for our sins, finally and completely. Do we really understand how much He loves us!!

We often shy away from the word "love" maybe because it is misused by the world, the media, the film industry. It is seen as a feminist thing, a weakish feeling? A kiss or two? A sexual thing or at least a connotation thereof? Search the word "love" in the bible and you will be floored at how many times it appears.

When the Lord could not face the sinning people He created and loved (Gen 6 verse 6), He was sorry. I came across a number of explanations of the word sorry. The following explanations caught my attention in terms of this statement in Scripture, that He was "sorry": "**Sorrowful, disheartened,** broken-hearted, heartbroken, inconsolable, grief-stricken"

This is how someone would feel who loves another and is disappointed by that person's loveless actions, would it not? God had an expectation from what He created. He wanted man to understand Love!! To be like Him, a lover!! When man sinned greatly He could not face this terrible attitude of man, killing each other and hating each other. It was too much, just to overwhelming and He became sorrowful, disheartened, broken-hearted, heartbroken, inconsolable, grief-stricken (sorry).He was in such a state that He decided, no this is not working, this is not what I wanted, not what was in My heart. *Gen 6:6 And the LORD was sorry that He had made man on the earth, <u>and He was grieved in His heart.</u>*

God then decided to destroy man from the face of the earth. Yet He is a God of love and one man, just one man, caught His attention and He decided, no. I will not completely destroy man...He saw this righteous man Noah who loved God and this one man gave Him hope, even though he knew man would still sin greatly. God reminded Himself of His own promises and He still desired that someone share in His love, His glory. I am making assumptions here with respect to the Lord but it is what I gather from what I find in scripture. We are discussing the love of the Lord and it is in this context that I share with you the reader my understanding of what God was doing and why. But why would God tell us what happened in His heart? Why share this difficult to understand event?

Is it not to tell us how much He loved us from the beginning? When he eventually destroyed the human race, except for Noah and his family, it was also too difficult for God to bear and He decided not to do this again (Gen 8 verse 11). God knew that sin still lurked in the shadows and was even with Noah in the ark, but He decided to accept man's utter sinfulness and inability to be sinless. *Gen 8:21 And the LORD smelled the soothing aroma; and the LORD said to Himself, "I will never again curse the ground on account of man, for the intent of man's heart is evil from his youth; and I will never again destroy every living thing, as I have done.*

God decided to allow sin to have its way by choice because he loved His creation. He loves us so much!! He was willing to suffer the mess we make in order to give us time to repent and come to Him through the cross. He decided to this time round, carry the (sorrowful) burden of man's utter deceit. His love won the day in His heart?

This demonstration of the love God has for us all is just so absolutely captivating, so outside our own experiences!

Paul made a very precious statement and a declaration of what he calls a mystery, the similarity of the loving relationship between a man and his wife (male and female) and Christ (The Anointed One) and his church (the bride). *Eph 5:31 FOR THIS CAUSE A MAN SHALL LEAVE HIS FATHER AND MOTHER, AND SHALL CLEAVE TO HIS WIFE; AND THE TWO SHALL BECOME ONE FLESH.*
Eph 5:32 This mystery is great; **but I am speaking with reference to Christ and the church.**

The Songs Of Solomon is generally seen as an allegory of the relationship between Jesus Christ and His bride. It also clearly depicts what the relationship between a husband and his wife should be. I am not going to debate the various interpretations of this beautiful book in the bible. The Jewish rabbis, from the latter part of the 1st century AD down to our own day, taught that the poem celebrates a spiritual love, Yahweh being the bridegroom and Israel the bride. Canticles was supposed to be a vivid record of the loving relationship between Israel and her Lord from the Exodus on to the New Covenant or Testament. The Songs of Solomon is read by the Jews at Passover, which celebrates Yahweh's choice of Israel to be His bride. I am following this allegory but in the context of the New Testament where the bride is an inclusive bride as: *There is neither Jew nor Greek, there is neither slave nor free man, there is neither male nor female; for you are all one in Christ Jesus (Gal_3:28). For there is no distinction between Jew and Greek; for the same Lord is Lord of all, abounding in riches for all who call upon Him*

(Rom_10:12). It also confirms what the Spirit is revealing to me and surprisingly, this revelation (to me) starts with King David at his old age.

Now King David was old, advanced in age; and they covered him with clothes, but he could not keep warm. 2 So his servants said to him, "Let them seek a young virgin for my lord the king, and let her attend the king and become his nurse; and let her lie in your bosom, that my lord the king may keep warm." (1Ki 1:1)

3 So they searched for a beautiful girl throughout all the territory of Israel, and found Abishag the Shunammite, and brought her to the king. 4 And the girl was very beautiful; and she became the king's nurse and served him, but the king did not cohabit with her. (The name Shunammite means "favourite, resting place, quiet).

In Songs of Solomon we read that the girl here is a Shulammite. Many scholars assume the Shulammite and the Shunammite are the same. As Solomon knew about Abishag, that she was very beautiful and a virgin, it may have been her beauty and personality or the actual facts that she served David but stayed a virgin (pure)? that perhaps motivated Songs of Solomon? The two names have the same meaning and in 2 Kings 4 we read that the place the Shunammite came from is called Shunem. (The inhabitants could have been Israelites as this was one of the cities given to Issachar, one of the 12 sons of Jacob, that is, Israel).

We read that the Shunammite was to keep the king warm (happy) and serve him (take care of). If these two are the same girl, (Abishag) it projects a beautiful picture and underline a spiritual truth that is undeniably awesome. Let me explain what I believe the Spirit revealed to me concerning the Shunammite/Shulammite.

The relationship between the king and the girl is pure, there is no lust after her as David would possibly create a massive problem if there was another heir to the throne. She is there purely to make the king "happy". She was to bring "life" through her love for the king (willing to serve). She is so beautiful that Adonijah the king's son, asks for her hand at King David's death (from king Solomon). He had other motives as well so Solomon had him killed.

In Songs of Solomon we read that this Shulammite (her name is not given) represents the bride (portraying the church) of King Solomon (portraying Christ the Bridegroom). She loves the bridegroom as the church should love Jesus and He loves her as His bride even though she struggles to understand Him.

Now what the Lord further showed me is this:

We have a distorted understanding and therefore a blockage in receiving the love the Lord has for us and the love He requires from us. Jesus love for the Father is demonstrated in His obedience unto death and His fierce indignation when the Temple was desecrated by the money lenders and greed of the sellers, amongst others. Now hear the Love the Lord has for His bride, you and me:.000

Son 4:1 "How beautiful you are, my darling, How beautiful you are!

Son 6:4 "You are as beautiful as Tirzah, my darling, As lovely as Jerusalem, As awesome as an army with banners.

Son 7:6 "How beautiful and how delightful you are, My love, with all your charms!

Son 4:9 "You have made my heart beat faster, my sister, my bride; You have made my heart beat faster with a single glance of your eyes, With a single strand of your necklace.

Deu_23:5 "Nevertheless, the LORD your God was not willing to listen to Balaam, but the LORD your God turned the curse into a blessing for you because the LORD your God loves you.

2Ch_2:11 Then Huram, king of Tyre, answered in a letter sent to Solomon: "Because the LORD loves His people, He has made you king over them."

Joh 16:27 for the Father Himself loves you, because you have loved Me, and have believed that I came forth from the Father.

Joh_14:23 Jesus answered and said to him, "If anyone loves Me, he will keep My word; and My Father will love him, and We will come to him, and make Our abode with him.

Then, all of a sudden the bridegroom is not there and the Shulammite eventually came to realise he has gone. The bride is alone!

 Son 3:1 *"On my bed night after night I sought him Whom my soul loves; I sought him but did not find him. : 2 'I* **must arise now and go about the city;**

In the streets and in the squares I must seek him whom my soul loves.' *I sought him but did not find him. 3 "The watchmen who make the rounds in the city found me, And I said, 'Have you seen him whom my soul loves?'*

This call I received with so many scriptures affirming that the Lord is hiding (calling) so that we must seek Him. We must seek His love! Fellowship of a Songs of Solomon kind!!

We are so busy with other matters we did not even notice His disappearance. Singing, dancing, bazaars, preaching and ministering, which is all good stuff, has taken the place of true abiding, loving fellowship. We have even become so enamored by some very spiritual members amongst us that they have taken the place of our Lords first place!

The bridegroom loves the shulammite (bride) even though she (Abishag…as we assume she is the same girl we read of in Kings) was rejected..(Abishag means "my father errs") , her father a wanderer who sinned greatly, her skin blackened by the sun as she tended the sheep and worked in her brothers vineyards (So 1 verse 6) . They scorned her and pushed her away. She finds herself being chosen by the king as his bride and loved by him to such an extent that it captures her heart and she loves him also. When He disappears she searches him with a passion. Though she is rejected and of no repute (So 1 verse 7) the king finds her most beautiful. The Lord has only one image of His bride the church: Son 4:1 *"How beautiful you are, my darling, How beautiful you are! Your eyes are like doves behind your veil; Your hair is like a flock of goats That have descended from Mount Gilead"* Please read the Hosea passage of scripture above again.

The bridegroom goes on and says: *Son 4:7 "You are altogether beautiful, my darling, And there is no blemish in you. 8 "Come with me from Lebanon, my bride, May you come with me from Lebanon. Journey down from the summit of Amana, From the summit of Senir and Hermon, From the dens of lions, From the mountains of leopards. 9 "You have made my heart beat faster, my sister, my bride; You have made my heart beat faster with a single glance of your eyes, With a single strand of your necklace. 10 "How beautiful is your love, my sister, my bride! How much better is your love than wine, And the fragrance of your oils Than all kinds of spices! 11 "Your lips, my bride, drip honey; Honey and milk are under your tongue, And the fragrance of your garments is like the fragrance of Lebanon. 12 "A garden locked is my sister, my bride, A rock garden locked, a spring sealed up.*

Even though the church has been scorched by the sun, has sinned many times and who's fathers are sinners, rejected by the world, He loves her tenderly. He describes every part of her as lovely, from her lips, her hair, her breasts, her whole body He loves. Even though her work is seen by the world as of no value, He values her. In Egypt a shepherd was looked down upon. *Gen 46:34 that you shall say, 'Your servants have been keepers of livestock from our youth even until now, both we and our fathers,' that you may live in the land of Goshen; for every shepherd is loathsome to the Egyptians." (Abishag* was a shepherd)

The world does not understand the true church. The bride is not to be part of the world. The Lord loves her and nothing else matters. When the bridegroom disappears she immediately goes looking for him. She (the Shulammite) cannot live without him. The church, the bride, likewise cannot live without Him, His love, His forgiveness, His compassion and kindness, His presence! Should He withdraw for a while, the church will know if the church really loves Him, and will seek Him. Where she came from (the Shulammite) she received only rejection, the scorching of the sun, hardship. The church cannot survive without her Bridegroom.

The bridegroom withdraws for a time, I believe, for a reason. He wants her to find out how much she loves Him. She needs to know that she really loves him. *Son 5:8 "I adjure you, O daughters of Jerusalem, If you find my beloved, As to what you will tell him: For I am lovesick."*

It is often when a loved one is not present that we begin to realise we long after that one's presence. We realise the true value of the one we seek to have fellowship with again. Jesus was with His disciples for 3 years then suddenly He tells them he is going away and that where He is going they cannot go. All of a sudden they had to imagine a life without Him and it hit them hard. When He is eventually forcefully removed from them by evil men, whipped with whips' that tore the flesh from His body and crucified before their very eyes, they were devastated. Most of them went back to what they did before meeting Jesus. Until, until someone says they saw Him, Mary saw Him, and a glimmer of hope returns. He then appears to them and I can imagine the hearts restored, the hope restored, the love restored, the fellowship restored.

However, He was going to leave them again but now he promises to send someone who will be with them forever and satisfy every longing of their souls. Now we read in Songs of Solomon the following very significant words:

Chapter 4 deals with the bride *(Son 4:10 "How beautiful is your love, my sister, my bride! ...) and then he says:* Son 4:15 "You are a garden spring, A well of fresh water, And streams flowing from Lebanon." 4:16 "Awake, O north wind, And come, wind of the south; Make my garden (the bride) breathe out fragrance, Let its spices be wafted abroad. May my beloved come into his garden and eat its choice fruits!" This speaks of the Holy Spirit the bride needs to bring forth that fragrance of love, acceptance, life and forgiveness.

The church as the bride must become fully aware again of its position, its need and its task on earth today. It must know it is loved with a love so pure and holy and powerful, that Holy Spirit will provide everything and satisfy every longing of the human heart.

Joh 15:12 This is My commandment, That ye love one another, as I have loved you.

13 Greater love hath no man than this that a man lay down his life for his friends.
14 Ye are My friends, if ye do whatsoever I command you.

Wine farmers in the Stellenbosch (South Africa) area plant rose trees at every row of vineyard as rose trees will immediately indicate the presence of fungi first, assisting the vine growers to take action before the vineyard is infested. Rose trees are also quick to indicate too little or too much water, fertilisers, etc. Likewise our agape love will immediately show us that there is an attack and that we should take corrective action.

My wife was given some rose trees and since then we have learned so much from them. We added to and replaced some over the years and today all of them have full fragrance characteristics and beautiful flowers. When too much or too little water is given, they respond very quickly. Too much or too little fertiliser will show. What is amaising is that they respond very quickly, sometimes within a couple of hours or a day or two. Love or the lack thereof in our hearts will very quickly indicate our spiritual condition!

Love also compels us to go deeper, to know more, to know the depth, height, width and breadth of it. In Eph. 3 verses 17 to 19 we read that the love of Christ surpasses knowledge! It is by His love that we are by faith filled up to all the fullness of God. *Eph 3:17 so that Christ may dwell in your hearts through faith; and that you, being rooted and grounded in love, 18 may be able to comprehend with all the saints what is the breadth and length and height and depth, 19 and to know the love of Christ which surpasses knowledge, that you may be filled up to all the fullness of God.*

If we are being led through life by a love for the Lord, we will continually by drawn to Him to know His fullness! The text above implies that we can actually know Him that well!! (As far as humanly possible and progressively so). But do we poses this love?
The Lord addresses this lacking attribute and fruit of the Spirit first (Rev. 2…letter to the angel at Ephesus), lacking in first love!! Ephesus means "Full Purpose" and prophetically it seems the Lord is saying that first love is required to reach our full purpose as a pastor, preacher, etc.

Then, as if to further emphasise the very role and importance of agape love, 1 Cor. 13 verse 1 states: *If I speak with the tongues of men and of angels, but do not have love, I have become a noisy gong or a clanging cymbal. And if I have the gift of prophecy, and know all mysteries and all knowledge; and if I have all faith, so as to remove mountains, but do not have love, I am nothing.*

Our salvation is a pure act of love from the Father and our creator God in heaven. There is no way our own efforts could deserve this. The law clearly states that he who trespasses any one of the commandments shall die. Every one of us who claim to be Christian should keep in mind that the Lord Himself decided to save us through the cross of Calvary. It was and still is an act of love!! Jesus is and appears as the Lamb of God in heaven even though He is the Lion as well!! The woman who was thrown at His feet for condemnation by the law receives His pardon in love: *Joh_8:11 And she said, "No one, Lord." And Jesus said, "Neither do I condemn you; go your way. From now on sin no more.*

Revelation 2 and 3 addresses us, the pastors and preachers, spiritual leaders who oversee the flock in one way or another. This is the message that needs to be heard, and my prayer is that we will hear the word of the Lord today, that we are addressed by the One who: *Rev 1:14 And His head and His hair were white like white wool, like snow; and His eyes were like a flame of fire....*

Rev 2:4 'But I have this against you, that you have left your first love.

The love required here is therefore much more than just being thankful and happy that we are saved and going to heaven! It is far more than just saying "I love You". It is a love as the Shulammite has for her lover, the king! One that made her seek him until she finds him. Don Basham wrote a book called Deliver us from Evil and therein he explained how he found himself drifting away from the Lord. It cost him two weeks two hours per day early in the morning struggling in prayer, until he "found" the Lord again. Then the Lord led Don Basham to teach the congregation to pray and they experienced revival in that church!

There are an increasing number of Christians (including spiritual leaders) who are choosing to walk in their full purpose in the Lord. They have counted the cost and have decided to pay the price of sacrificing their lives, dreams and wills in order to know, love and obey the Lord. Many are praying without ceasing and are in earnest with God. There are many who do not seek the praises of men but seek to find what is pleasing to the Lord. These are experiencing much persecution and are misunderstood and sometimes maligned by brothers and sisters who do not understand and unfortunately lack the wisdom required.

I believe there is now an urgent call for spiritual leaders in the church (and the church) to likewise stir up their spiritual fire and zeal for the Lord, to equip and protect the elect of the Lord in these turbulent times. It is more who He is in us than who we are in Him that needs attention today!! We need to really know Him, love Him and adore Him. (Mat 22:37 and *He said to him, "you shall **love** the Lord your God with all your heart, and with all your soul, and with all your mind.'*)

The heart needs a facelift, yes, as David prayed, a new heart. What has happened that we have been so deceived into thinking that if we do things we choose to do for the Lord, we are pleasing Him? Dear spiritual leader, we should not be ignorant but understand what the will of the Lord is (Eph. 5:17). Have we ever thought why it does not say "you shall obey", or "you shall serve..." but you shall **love**? We have a problem with love in that we always want to add something. We believe it cannot be just love!

There is more to life than just loving, is it not? The truth is, nothing is of any worth whatsoever without love. Love will follow Jesus. Love will obey Jesus. Love will honour the Lord. It took nearly 2000 years plus, up to the cross of Calvary, for the Lord to teach us what love really is.

A close walk with the Lord over a period of time begins to reflect on our countenance because we are spending time in His presence!

It also reflects in our speech and our body language. My experience of such followers of Jesus is that they portray a humbleness and gentleness as well as perfect peace that makes you feel comfortable and loved in their presence! My spirit just about leaps for joy in me and this is no illusion. The church must be such a body, even foreigners should be able to feel it: Joh 13:35 *"By this all men will know that you are My disciples, if you have love for one another.*

It is the flow of godly love between us and the Lord and between ourselves that will impact the world more than any powerful teaching or preaching would!! I am not saying preaching and teaching is not necessary, in fact they are very necessary. How else would we know the will and plans God has for us? It is bringing the gospel with the heart of love that will impact others positively. Joh 15:12 *"This is My commandment, that you love one another, just as I have loved you.*

1Pe 4:8 Above *all, keep fervent in your love for one another, because love covers a multitude of sins. 9 Be hospitable to one another without complaint.* Phm 1:7 For *I have come to have much joy and comfort in your love, because the hearts of the saints have been refreshed through you, brother.* Phm 1:5 because *I hear of your love, and of the faith which you have toward the Lord Jesus, and toward all the saints;* This is Love speaking!

This is so crucial that Paul penned down 1Co 13:1 If *I speak with the tongues of men and of angels, but do not have love, I have become a noisy gong or a clanging cymbal.*

Jesus loves His own and comforts them with these words of love:

Joh 14:1 *"Let not your heart be troubled; believe in God, believe also in Me.*
2 "In My Father's house are many dwelling places; if it were not so, I would have told you; for I go to prepare a place for you. 3 "And if I go and prepare a place for you, I will come again, and

receive you to Myself; that where I am, there you may be also. Jesus loves us to such an extent that it brings Him to promise us eternal life in heaven! He even says, "where I am"!!

Joh 15:13 *"Greater love has no one than this, that one lay down his life for his friends. 14 "You are My friends, if you do what I command you. 15 "No longer do I call you slaves, for the slave does not know what his master is doing; but I have called you friends, for all things that I have heard from My Father I have made known to you. 16 "You did not choose Me, but*

I chose you, and appointed you, that you should go and bear fruit, and that your fruit should remain, that whatever you ask of the Father in My name, He may give to you.

A dear friend of the Lord was so blessed due to him and his family being spared of certain death that he decided to show his love and reverence by immediately worshiping the Lord and thanked him for saving his life and that of his family. The Lord was so blessed by this that He decided there and then, through just this one man's thankfulness, to save his whole race. This man was Noah: Gen 8:20 *Then Noah built an altar to the LORD, and took of every clean animal and of every clean bird and offered burnt offerings on the altar. 21 And the LORD smelled the soothing aroma; and the LORD said to Himself, "I will never again curse the ground on account of man, for the intent of man's heart is evil from his youth; and I will never again destroy every living thing, as I have done.*

The church needs to be a place of love for the Lord first and then one another, extending to the world at large. This love was poured out into our hearts at our rebirth into His kingdom and should grow exponentially to our continued fellowship with Him and each other. The gifts of the Holy Spirit, which is given to serve one another, is to operate from a heart where love rules.

Chris Hamman

WALKING IN THE SPIRIT

2Co 3:17, 18 Now the Lord is the Spirit: and where the Spirit of the Lord is, there is liberty. But we all, with open face beholding as in a glass the glory of the Lord, are changed into the same image from glory to glory, even as by the Spirit of the Lord.

Being made to realise our critical need of Holy Spirit as a man with impaired sight needs a pair of glasses to bring into proper focus what he reads, I felt it imperative that we discuss this issue a little.

Have you ever come across these verses and wondered a bit on their meaning:
Pro_14:12 There is a way which seems right to a man, But its end is the way of death. Pro_16:25 There is a way which seems right to a man, But its end is the way of death.

This must be very important as King Solomon uses this word twice! Reading this I was reminded of the following word: *2 Co_3:6 who also made us adequate as servants of a new covenant, not of the letter, but of the Spirit; for the letter kills, but the Spirit gives life.*

Trying to understand God`s word with the mind alone is not possible. This I believe is the way of man which leads to death! I felt it important therefore to discuss this issue here as well. Few realize that we are totally helpless without Him. (*Joh_3:5 Jesus answered, Verily, verily, I say unto thee, Except a man be born of water and of the Spirit, he cannot enter into the kingdom of God.*).

A certain pastor was sitting outside a church in his car, contemplating the word he had to bring. Fear and uncertainty flooded his mind as he realised the awesomeness of the task ahead. His dear wife was seated in church, waiting for him to bring the message. She left her seat and went out to him and said to him: My love, the Lord has just told me to give you Acts 1 verse 8: ....*you shall receive power when the Holy Spirit has come upon you and you shall be My witness...* He left the car encouraged and did what he had to do with boldness.

Once I was challenged by a pastor to prove to him that Paul preached on the Holy Spirit. I promised to pray about it and was led to these verses: Gal 3:1: *You foolish Galatians, who has bewitched you, before whose eyes Jesus Christ was publicly portrayed as crucified? 2 This is the only thing I want to find out from you: did you receive the Spirit by the works of the Law, or by hearing with faith? 3 Are you so foolish? Having begun by the Spirit, are you now being perfected by the flesh?*

Paul was completely taken by surprise, hence his word choice:"who has bewitched you". The truth is that when you move away from being led by the Spirit of the Lord, "having begun" you and I fall back to law. This is why we want to tell (preach) people to abide by the word of God in the flesh, instead of relying on the Holy Spirit to teach (There is no vacuum in between) *Jer 31:34 And they shall teach no more every man his neighbour, and every man his brother, saying, Know the LORD: for they shall all know me, from the least of them unto the greatest of them, saith the LORD.*

Please bear with me as I try to unravel, amongst others, this very, very important issue (of being led by the Spirit and not the flesh in our teaching and preaching).

<u>Joh 14:26</u> *But the Comforter, which is the Holy Ghost, whom the Father will send in my name, he shall teach you all things, and*

bring all things to your remembrance, whatsoever I have said unto you.

<u>Luk 12:12</u> *For the Holy Ghost shall teach you in the same hour what ye ought to say.*

<u>Heb 8:11</u> *And they shall not teach every man his neighbour, and every man his brother, saying, Know the Lord: for all shall know me, from the least to the greatest.*

<u>1Jn 2:27</u> *But the anointing which ye have received of him abideth in you, and ye need not that any man teach you: but as the same anointing teacheth you of all things, and is truth, and is no lie, and even as it hath taught you, ye shall abide in him.*

The only point I would like to make here dear reader is the fact that the flesh will always strive to teach in its own power and understanding if the Spirit is not in control. (*Rom 7:23 But I see another law in my members, warring against the law of my mind,*) The enemy knows this and will always contend with the Spirit filled saint and the move of the Spirit. He will always try to influence the flesh to become involved and to eventually take control.....even to the point of utter confusion...as in the church in Corinth where Paul had to bring order. As a leader in the body of Christ we need to be constantly aware of this but we should not fear walking in the Spirit.

This perverted gospel the Galatians were hearing from others clearly held no revelation of Christ. There was no Christ-life in it. In Rev 2 and 3 the word "tolerate" stands out like a sore thumb. .According to the Cambridge Advanced Learner's Dictionary & Thesaurus tolerate means "to accept behaviour and beliefs that are different from your own, although you might not agree with or approve of them" Putting this in context with Revelations it could read: "to accept behaviour and beliefs that are different from what

Jesus taught, although you realise or know they might not agree with His teachings"?

To Timothy Paul wrote:

1Ti 4:13 Until *I come, give attention to the public reading of Scripture, to exhortation and teaching. 14 Do not neglect the **spiritual gift** within you, which was bestowed upon you through prophetic utterance with the laying on of hands by the presbytery.*

What gifts are Paul referring to?

*1Co 12:1 Now concerning **spiritual gifts**, brethren, I do not want you to be unaware.*

1Co 12:8 For to one is given the word of wisdom through the Spirit, and to another the word of knowledge according to the same Spirit; 9 to another faith by the same Spirit, and to another gifts of healing by the one Spirit, 10 and to another the effecting of miracles, and to another prophecy, and to another the distinguishing of spirits, to another various kinds of tongues, and to another the interpretation of tongues. 11 But one and the same Spirit works all these things, distributing to each one individually just as He wills

Timothy is reminded that the Spirit is crucial to his ministry. Paul says: 2Co 3:6 *who also made us adequate as servants of a new covenant, not of the letter, but of the Spirit; for the letter kills,* **but the Spirit gives life.** I was shocked when I realised the truth that a religious spirit is actually anti-christ. It does not say anti-Jesus but anti-CHRIST, referring to the fact that Christ the Anointed One is targeted. It requires wisdom and discernment to see how deep this hatred of the spirit of Anti-Christ is for the bride and the Bridegroom, how he tirelessly works both in the world and in the church to suppress the Anointing.

I would like the reader to know that what I bring requires a close walk with the Holy Spirit in order to understand and receive what I humbly share. *There seems to be a sense of divine mystery throughout the kingdom of God which is far beyond the mysteries that scientists discover running throughout the kingdom of nature* (AW Tozer. Whatever Happened to Worship)? Paul states: *But earnestly desire the greater gifts. And I show you a still more excellent way (*1Co 12:31).

I was asked to orientate and train a graduate student in what I was doing as a consultant for a large municipality. He was so excited about what he learned from me that he stated that this is what he actually was seeking and why he studied at university. My answer to him was that he will find that what he had experienced will enhance and bring into focus what he had studied. In a sense the Holy Spirit "enhances" – enlightens the written word. The written word is limited in bringing across God`s heart therefore we need Holy Spirit. He is actually the Teacher.

I have copied a portion of a word from Elaine Tavolacci <awordinseason@live.com> ....that was given in 2010 and is absolutely relevant to the message I believe I need to bring:

Quote
January 12, 2010
I am moving in these days mightily by My Spirit, which is moving from Sea to Sea, Nation to Nation for I am shaking My church, My body of followers, to wake up and be led of My spirit to benefit My Kingdom on earth. For I am the great I am, the Mighty God. Those who set aside their own kingdom and deny self will see an increase, yes a double portion of My presence and anointing.................................

For I am calling My servants to arise and shine and shake off the dust of the world and be led by My spirit for that is My desire for you to be My channels, my conduits of power. For I am raising up My army to possess the land, to take more territory for Me. Almighty army flowing in one accord, arm to arm fighting to promote My Kingdom on planet earth. Many shall be awaken from sleep to press into Me and I shall take them to heaven and give them marching orders for the battle of invading earth with heaven..

As My corporate church, flows in unity they shall see a Mighty Move of My presence with a mighty outpouring of signs and wonders and miracles. A people who desire to <u>be My conduits of love ministering to the poor, the needy the rejected and the sick, the widows, and the captives. I am raising up a body to flow in love, without pride and in humility to walk as I walked on planet earth</u>..

Yes with this shaking which will affect the way My corporate church functions, there will be a dying of self kingdoms. I am calling My church, My body of believers to go back to the book of Acts and meet, breaking bread and ministering to one another. I am calling a people who will not run from Me but come to Me daily and pray and seek My face for then you shall see much healing, restoration and revival in your land..

I am moving and shaking individuals and My whole body to press into Me in deeper intimacy, worship, praise and prayer to seek Me the one and only God of planet earth. I am raising up My army to flow in My double portion presence and anointing. So receive this shaking, don't fight it surrender, come to Me, the one who gives you power and authority to sound My Trumpet and declare I am alive and walking on planet earth through My army who lays down their lives to promote My Glory!
   -   End quote -

Now He said that He will send the Holy Spirit who will teach and guide us because He wants us to be where He is, in Heaven!! He died to be able to promise this to us!! Without missing a beat over many years God sent His Son: Joh 3:16 *"For God so loved the world, that He gave His only begotten Son, that whoever believes in Him should not perish, but have eternal life.* After Adam and

Eve sinned and grieved Father God, Noah came and lived righteously, was given an awesome promise by God and God even confirmed it with the rainbow in the sky!! One act of love, one act of pure thankfulness and reverence by one man pleased God even though He said: *"for the intent of man's heart is evil from his youth"*.

Psa 148 *Kings of the earth and all peoples; Princes and all judges of the earth; Both young men and virgins; Old men and children. Let them praise the name of the LORD, For His name alone is exalted; His glory is above earth and heaven.*

Joh 1:1 In *the beginning was the Word, and the Word was with God, and the Word was God. He was in the beginning with God. All things came into being by Him, and apart from Him nothing came into being that has come into being. In Him was life, and the life was the light of men. And the light shines in the darkness, and the darkness did not comprehend it.*

Rev 1 And *I turned to see the voice that was speaking with me. And having turned I saw seven golden lampstands; and in the middle of the lampstands one like a son of man, clothed in a robe reaching to the feet, and girded across His breast with a golden girdle. And His head and His hair were white like white wool, like snow; and His eyes were like a flame of fire; and His feet were like burnished bronze, when it has been caused to glow in a furnace, and His voice was like the sound of many waters.*

Chris Hamman

THE ARK OF THE LORD

Mat 12:6 *"But I say to you, that something greater than the temple is here.*

The Ark represented the presence of the Lord amongst His people before Messiah came and was holy: *Lev_16:2 The LORD said to Moses: "Tell your brother Aaron that he shall not enter at any time into the holy place inside the veil, before the mercy seat which is on the ark, or he will die; for I will appear <u>in the cloud</u> over the mercy seat.*

Ark actually means container, coffin or box in Hebrew. It contained the tablets of the Ten Commandments, the staff of Aaron and a pot of manna. The Lord would appear above the mercy seat, yet He was not contained in it. It had no power or inherent holiness. It was God who chose to come down as He planned, commanded and chose to do. The above verse clearly states ...."For I will appear over the mercy seat". It was His mercy shown to Israel in appearing to Moses and giving Moses instructions regarding the nation Israel, the people of God (Exod 25 verse 22).

When Moses entered the Holy of Holies, what he, and later the high priest, experienced was, however, past awesome...the light of God shining on the golden Ark and mercy seat with the cherubim facing each other and the interwoven cherubim in the fabric of the curtains shining like stars or angels round about.

He could not see anything else as the curtains blocked out the outside world and he would be conscious only of the colourful

 display of glory created by the light of the Lord and reflected by the cherubim and the golden Ark (Rev. 5 verse 11, Rev. 4 verse 3 and Ezek. 1 verses 27 and 28). The Lord then instructed Moses or the high priest who had to convey the will of the Lord to the people. Can we imagine this absolute holy and awesome event? In the presence of the most holy God, the creator of everything?

When Moses entered the tabernacle the Cloud descended and hovered over the Tent of Meeting, covering it completely. I believe this cloud is the Holy Spirit (water).

When Moses appeared before the Lord, his face shined similar to the glory or light within the holy of holies. He had to cover his face when he came out because the people were afraid of him (Exod. 34 verses 34 and 35).

The Ark was to Israel the presence and the power of God. During the time of their desert wanderings the light that emanated from between the cherubim on the mercy seat could be seen partially and reminded the Israelis that God was in their midst.

Somehow the ark got lost during the invasion of Babylon's Nebuchadnezzar. There are many theories as to what happened to the ark and its reappearance in heaven: (Rev_11:19 *And the temple of God which is in heaven was opened; and the ark of His covenant appeared in His temple, and there were flashes of lightning and sounds and peals of thunder and an earthquake and a great hailstorm.*

I believe the most significant scripture regarding the future of the ark is found in Jeremiah: Jer_3:16 *"And it shall be in those days when you are multiplied and increased in the land," declares the LORD, "they shall say no more, 'The ark of the covenant of the*

LORD.' *And it shall not come to mind, nor shall they remember it, nor shall they miss it, nor shall it be made again.*

Jeremiah 7 verse 4 states: *"Do not trust in deceptive words, saying, 'This is the temple of the LORD, the temple of the LORD, the temple of the LORD.'* Belonging to a church means little without the heart being rent and filled with righteousness (verses 5 onwards). Mat 12:6 *"But I say to you, that something greater than the temple is here.*

Dear pastor, reverent, teacher, preacher, prophet, etc. as we by faith (through our mediator Jesus Christ) enter heaven by prayer to appear before Him (the ark in heaven) He will instruct us and the glory of the Lord (Holy Spirit) will surround us, empower us, give us again ears to hear and eyes to see! If we would spend time in prayer with the burning desire to know His will and to enjoy His presence, we will find that our "face", our heart, shine with His presence (Rev 5 verse 10 *And He has made us unto our God kings and priests and we shall reign on earth* (Isaiah 22 verse 22).

The explanation that I find acceptable as to why the ark "reappears" in heaven (Rev.11 verse 10) is that it refocuses our prayers from earth (Tabernacle on earth) to heaven. We are encouraged to enter into His presence as it was originally given to only the high priest! Just as the priest did, we should get our "instructions and guidance" from heaven, from God Himself as we by faith enter and experience His presence, His glory. Just as the priest had to cleanse himself we must by faith in Jesus who cleanses us daily, enter and appear before Him:
Heb. 2:9 But we do see Him who has been made for a little while lower than the angels, namely, Jesus, because of the suffering of death <u>crowned with glory and honor,</u> that by the grace of God He might taste death for everyone.

We are invited to come with holy boldness: (*Heb_4:16 Let us therefore come boldly unto the throne of grace that we may obtain mercy, and find grace to help in time of need*). Jesus Himself prayed for this to happen: Joh 17:24 *"Father, I desire that they also, whom Thou hast given Me, be with Me where I am, in order that they may behold My glory, which Thou hast given Me; for Thou didst love Me before the foundation of the world"* This word is written in the present tense. Now, today.

Heb. 1 verse 1 states emphatically that God now speaks through His Son, the Word of God, whereas he spoke in many ways to us during the old covenant. When we appear before the throne of the Lord, He is there to intercede for us as our high priest (*Heb 3:1*

Therefore, holy brethren, partakers of a heavenly calling, consider Jesus, the Apostle and High Priest of our confession). Jesus is there, representing the "Bread of Life", the Sacrifice (the Lamb that was slain), the Laver (Wash us by His Word).

What is more, Jesus made us family *Heb 2:11 For both He who sanctifies and those who are sanctified are all from one Father; for which reason He is not ashamed to call them brethren,*

12 saying, "I will proclaim thy name to My brethren, in the midst of the congregation I will sing thy praise."

Dear pastor, preacher, teacher, prophet of the most high God, we are called very specifically to come near to Him today. I believe that when we come today, the cloud that covered the ark, the most Holy Spirit of God will not only cover but fill us up to overflowing, again and again as we enter boldly, daily, to hear from Him, be empowered by Him and sent by Him. It is His ordained will for us to be full of His Spirit, completely in His right hand so that He may sow us into a hurting world today. The children of God, the flock, has gone astray and we are called to "bring them back"!! The five-fold ministry He ordained to operate in His church must be revived and the child of God empowered filled and effective again. Love must be the hallmark of the church, the bride of Christ.

And the Lord says Come: Rev_22:17 And *the Spirit and the bride say, "Come." And let the one who hears say, "Come." And let the one who is thirsty come; let the one who wishes take the water of life without cost.*

Chris Hamman

ENTERING HEAVEN

Mat 18:3 and said, Verily I say unto you, Except ye turn, and become as little children, ye shall in no wise enter into the kingdom of heaven (KJV).

In Hebrews verse 10 to 12 of chapter 8 we see that the prophecy of Jer. 31 verse 34 is fulfilled. I believe that these verses explains who is teaching us (I, that is, God Himself) What it does not appear to explain is the how? So we are told who and the question remains, how?

Heb 8:10 For this is the covenant that I will make with the house of Israel after those days, saith the Lord; I will put my laws into their mind, and write them in their hearts: and I will be to them a God, and they shall be to me a people:
Heb 8:11 And they shall not teach every man his neighbour, and every man his brother, saying, Know the Lord: for all shall know me, from the least to the greatest.
Heb 8:12 For I will be merciful to their unrighteousness, and their sins and their iniquities will I remember no more.

Faith come by hearing the Truth so it is clear someone must speak or preach it. So we have this problem that God was not satisfied with His preachers and teachers and proclaimed that He now will do it Himself...How? He did not leave it to man to bring the Truth anymore! So how is He to do this Himself?

Here is the answer, I believe:

Act 1:8 But ye shall receive power, after that the Holy Ghost is come upon you: and ye shall be witnesses unto me both in Jerusalem, and in all Judaea, and in Samaria, and unto the uttermost part of the earth. John 15 verse 26 But when the Comforter is come, whom I will send unto you from the Father, even the Spirit of truth, which procedeth from the Father, he shall testify of me: and chapter 16 verse 13: *Howbeit when he, the Spirit of truth, is come, he will guide you into all truth: for he shall not speak of himself; but whatsoever he shall hear, that shall he speak: and he will shew you things to come*

(Please read the testimony of Belma Vavi in Annexure D before continuing)

God chooses through whom He will speak:

Act 1:24 And they prayed, and said, "Thou, Lord, who knowest the hearts of all men, show which one of these two Thou hast chosen 25 to occupy this ministry and apostleship from which Judas turned aside to go to his own place." 26 And they drew lots for them, and the lot fell to Matthias; and he was numbered with the eleven apostles.

Act 2:17 'AND IT SHALL BE IN THE LAST DAYS,' God says, 'THAT I WILL POUR FORTH OF MY SPIRIT UPON ALL MANKIND; AND YOUR SONS AND YOUR DAUGHTERS SHALL PROPHESY, AND YOUR YOUNG MEN SHALL SEE VISIONS, AND YOUR OLD MEN SHALL DREAM DREAMS; 18 EVEN UPON MY BONDSLAVES, BOTH MEN AND WOMEN, I WILL IN THOSE DAYS POUR FORTH OF MY SPIRIT And they shall prophesy.

Act 4:8. Then Peter, filled with the Holy Spirit, said to them, "Rulers and elders of the people, We see here that the Holy Spirit empowers Peter to boldly proclaim the truth.

1Ti 1:18 This command I entrust to you, Timothy, my son, in accordance with the prophecies previously made concerning you, that by them you may fight the good fight,

The Holy Spirit is the Voice of the Lord (John 16 verse 13) and we the leaders of the flock need to hear Him and convey what is said. We need to "go in" before the Lord in prayer and fasting and get our "instructions" from Him directly. We need to be filled with Him to speak and preach to ensure the message is from Him who promised that He will teach us Himself. Does that make sense? God speaks through His anointed angels/stars and they should be able to say "thus sayeth the Lord" We become a vessel and a vehicle or instrument in His right hand!! Because the Spirit is also in me the hearer, I will receive the truth, discerning by the Spirit that it is the truth.

Spiritual leader, we are to be the Voice of the Lord as He promised that he will teach us Himself. This is our awesome, holy responsibility!

However, in order for us to really receive what The Lord is about to pour out we need to be like children, like a child: *Luk 18:17 "Truly I say to you, whoever does not receive the kingdom of God like a child shall not enter it at all." Php 2:22 But you know of his proven worth that he served with me in the furtherance of the gospel <u>like a child serving his father.</u>*

As this requirement was voiced by Jesus Himself and the fact that He states: *"whoever does not receive the kingdom of God like a child **shall not** enter it at all"*, must catch our specific attention!!

David Markee, a world renowned worship leader and musician to whom the Lord had spoken a number of times to become more childlike in the past, recounts how the Lord taught him this awesome truth in his book "The Lost Glory". He visited the Toronto church where the Lord was doing a work that made headlines in the 1990s and he landed up between a number of exuberant Korean Christians. He was so offended by their visible expression of their love of the Lord that he decided to move and during the evening service, to go and sit somewhere else. I pick up the story from there and quote:

"This is too much. These people have gone over the top! So I got my coat and moved because I felt uncomfortable. The Lord was obviously trying to show me something though, because that evening though we were in a church of around 5000 people, I found myself sitting in the middle of them again! I had moved but so had they!

When it came to the prayer time, they all got out of their seats and ran down to the front and the Holy Spirit hit them. They all went down like ninepins in a big pile and continued to play like children, waving their arms about and laughing. At about 11h30pm I went up to the front of the stage and by this time there were about 20 of them lying on the floor in a heap. I noticed the lady I had seen kissing the air and looked at her on the floor. "Lord, this is too much I thought". One of the girls was saying "come to Jesus, come to Jesus, plenty of room, big house, big house, plenty of room for everybody, come in, come and play" and was kissing the air again and again. I felt offended in my heart but just then the Lord spoke to me asking "what is the matter?" Lord I said, Can't You see what they are doing? It's just childish.
"Yes it is childish and I love it"

I felt my heart break at that moment because I knew how far away I was from being childlike in God's presence. All my training and experience had led me to the point where I thought I had to be grown-up to serve the Lord. The Lord asked me whether I was prepared to be a child in His presence. I found it so difficult that I had a tremendous battle in my heart because there were people from my church attending the conference with me and watching me as their pastor! I eventually said "Yes Lord" took my jacket off and lay down in the middle of them, asking them to pray for me. It was the most fantastic thing I have ever done in my whole life! They prayed for everything they could think of and there was all this singing going on. They were tapping me, touching me, and absolutely assaulted me with prayer. They were praying with their bodies and their minds, throwing everything into this intersession. It was not dancing, singing or preaching, it was just physically interceding with everything they had. I had a glimpse of intersession like I had never seen before.

As the Koreans were praying for me, I had the sense that God was fulfilling his word to me. I had not banked on the method He would use, but who am I to question Him?

In the last 18 months or so God has started to release this same kind of prophetic intersession into some churches. I believe it is a direct result of childlike obedience.
End quote (David Markee ...The Lost Glory)

This awesome truth is often ignored because it does not fit in a society where social standing and self-pride is the norm. Spiritual leaders are lifted up by the congregation and esteemed as a "holy man of God". How difficult will it be for such a one to become childlike? Imagine the Pope or the Reverent becoming childlike!! Christlikeness is the ability to trust the Lord like a child, to respond to love like a child, to follow and obey Him like a child. The Lord would often make me do things that is not a "grown-up" sort of response, like asking me to kneel for no apparent reason in the midst of a group far younger than me! When I did he said , no ... lower, so I had to bend down further, then He said lower, and eventually I landed up on my knees with my head on the floor..!! The result was amasing but I felt very small when doing what He requested of me.

Adults have a tendency to become cynical with age, while a child has yet to be touched by the concerns of the world. But the older we get, the more "hurdles of doubts and concerns" we tend to place in front of us. These hurdles slow us down, knock us off stride, or make us give up completely in what should be a growing relationship with God.

Whereas an adult is more likely to give up the race, a child sees the prize at the finish line. As you near the end of your adult life, can you look forward as a child and say, as Paul did in 2 Timothy 4:7: *"I have fought the good fight, I have finished the race, and I have kept the faith."* Children don't have adult hurdles in their race with God. Childlike faith, along with childlike love, are an open road to God's heart.

What Qualities Does a Child Have?

- A child is innocent.
- A child is trusting.
- A child believes without complication.
- A child has not had time to allow the preconceived notions of the world to form his decision-making process.
- A child receives with joy, forgetting herself with light-hearted abandonment.
- A child is humble.
- A child is content in the little things.
- A child has the faith to move mountains.
- A child is awed by majestic splendor.
- A child takes to heart God's Word in all its simplicity.

Matthew 18:3: "Assuredly, I say to you, unless you change and become as little children, you will by no means enter the kingdom of heaven."

THE WILL OF GOD

Mat 6:10 'Thy *kingdom come. Thy will be done, On earth as it is in heaven.*

This has been the spoken word in prayer of many but do we understand what it means?

Of course, as we all know, we must study the scriptures, for they reveal the will of God for our actions and attitudes. To be filled with the knowledge of God's will, we must be filled with God's Word. God's Word is His will! Those who are ignorant of God's Word will be totally ignorant of God's will. Studying and living His word is a daily requirement yet I find many lack understanding. Knowledge of God's will is foundational in developing Christian conduct and character. There is no way we can fulfil God's will if we don't know what it is. The starting point for any Christian is understanding God's will for his life. How can a person obtain such knowledge? <u>The first step is to desire it</u>. Jeremiah 29:13 says, "And ye shall seek me, and find me, when ye shall search for me with all your heart." People ask the Lord for knowledge **of His will** but don't receive it because they aren't seeking with ALL THEIR HEART. No one who has ever sought the Lord with all his heart has ever been disappointed.

Doing the will of God is the life of heaven because God is there! He works His will without hindrance in all souls who are wholly yielded up to Him and wait upon Him (in faith). It is from God in heaven that this heavenly life of doing His will must come down and be carried and maintained in us in proportion to our waiting and our yielding to God.(God's Will: Our Dwelling Place – Andrew Murray).

God has ordained a way for us to be able to do His will. ..".*but when the Holy Spirit has come....*" and this is not only a once off as many teach but continuously, like the oil running from the tree of life!! Luk 11:13 *"If you then, being evil, know how to give good gifts to your children, how much more shall your heavenly Father give the Holy Spirit to those who ask Him?"*

Do we realise that life in the Lord is like being in heaven? Do we realise that rebirth places the converted in a supernatural environment? The following verses explains:

Heb 6:4 *For in the case of those who have once been enlightened and have tasted of the heavenly gift and have been made partakers of the Holy Spirit, 5 and have tasted the good word of God and the powers of the age to come,* Powers of the age to come!! In this way the baptism in the Holy Spirit is intended to be the gateway to the supernatural. It is not a goal but a way to walk...it is intended by God that thereafter the Spirit – baptised believer should <u>walk in the supernatural</u> in such a way that it will become "natural" so to speak.

If we would remove all the references to the supernatural in all of the 28 chapters of the book of Acts, not one will be left intact. You cannot experience any of the events that took place during the early church history without the supernatural (Andrew Murray). Unified love amongst the brethren that witnesses to the world that we belong to Him is a supernatural occurrence!! Speaking in tongues, singing and praying in the spirit is a supernatural occurrence. Acts 19 verse 11 states that God wrought special miracles by the hands of Paul. In Greek special means that type of miracle that does not happen every day. In the early church miracles were an everyday occurrence but some such as what Paul did caught the churches attention!

We need this supernatural ability. God's will is that we walk in the supernatural in order:

<u>To love Him and love one another:</u> Joh 17:23 *I in them, and Thou in Me, that they may be perfected in unity, that the world may know that Thou didst send Me, and didst love them, even as Thou didst love Me. Joh 13:34 "A new commandment I give to you, that you love one another, even as I have loved you, that you also love one another.*

<u>To witness:</u> Act 1:8 but *you shall receive power when the Holy Spirit has come upon you; and you shall be My witnesses both in Jerusalem, and in all Judea and Samaria, and even to the remotest part of the earth."*

<u>To pray:</u> Rom 8:26 And *in the same way the Spirit also helps our weakness; for we do not know how to pray as we should, but the Spirit Himself intercedes for us with groanings too deep for words; 27 and He who searches the hearts knows what the mind of the Spirit is, because He intercedes for the saints according to the will of God.*

<u>To teach: (learn</u>) Joh 14:26 *"But the Helper, the Holy Spirit, whom the Father will send in My name, He will teach you all things, and bring to your remembrance all that I said to you.*

<u>To exalt Jesus:</u> Act 2:33 *"Therefore having been exalted to the right hand of God, and having received from the Father the promise of the Holy Spirit, He has poured forth this which you both see and hear. 34 "For it was not David who ascended into heaven, but he himself says: 'THE LORD SAID TO MY LORD, "SIT AT MY RIGHT HAND, 35 UNTIL I MAKE THINE ENEMIES A FOOTSTOOL FOR THY FEET."'*
36 "Therefore let all the house of Israel know for certain that God has made Him both Lord and Christ--this Jesus whom you crucified." Joh 16:14 *"He shall glorify Me; for He shall take of Mine, and shall disclose it to you.*

<u>To guide us:</u> Joh 16:13 "But when He, the Spirit of truth, comes, He will guide you into all the truth; for He will not speak on His own initiative, but whatever He hears, He will speak; and He will disclose to you what is to come.

<u>To administer life (health and eternal resurrection)</u> Rom 8:10 And *if Christ is in you, though the body is dead because of sin, yet the spirit is alive because of righteousness. 11 But if the Spirit of Him who raised Jesus from the dead dwells in you, He who raised Christ Jesus from the dead will also give life to your mortal bodies through His Spirit who indwells you.*

<u>To be empowered:</u> 1Co 12:7 *But to each one is given the manifestation of the Spirit for the common good. 8 For to one is given the word of wisdom through the Spirit, and to another the word of knowledge according to the same Spirit;:9 to another faith by the same Spirit, and to another gifts of healing by the one Spirit, 10 and to another the effecting of miracles, and to another prophecy, and to another the distinguishing of spirits, to another various kinds of tongues, and to another the interpretation of tongues. 11 But one and the same Spirit works all these things, distributing to each one individually just as He wills.*

<u>To unify us as one:</u> 1Co 12:13 *For by one Spirit we were all baptized into one body, whether Jews or Greeks, whether slaves or free, and we were all made to drink of one Spirit. 14 For the body is not one member, but many.*

It is not earnest thought, clear understanding or strong desire that will bring us what we need (to do all His will) but, wait for it: UNCEASING PRAYER!! (God's Will: Our Dwelling Place – Andrew Murray).

The Lord uses these words actually saying His angels are not perfectly keeping God's will: "I have this against you...."
I believe we need to repent as spiritual leaders and decide to return to His right hand to be used, to allow Him, to yield to Him, to His Holy Spirit to let Him build the house!! Rom 2:4 Or *do you think*

lightly of the riches of His kindness and forbearance and patience, not knowing that the kindness of God leads you to repentance?

Refusing His Spirit to do as He pleases is a sin of such magnitude that all effort is vain. Are WE a growing church? Are converts added daily to the congregation? Are converts baptized in the Spirit and discipled to become gifted children of the Lord God? How is the love between brothers and sisters? Does it convince anyone in the world outside that members belong to and are followers of Jesus? <u>Are we lacking in a childlike love that is visible?</u> Do we allow people who have a jezebel spirit to control meetings, etc? Are our celebrations a real spiritual experience where the Lord manifests in different ways? After all, He said where two or three gather in My name I will be in their midst.

We have to desire and execute the will of the Lord!!

Chris Hamman

THE WILL OF GOD PART 2

The angel took much care in measuring the temple that had to be rebuilt in Ezekiel's day. Every room and pillar is described with measurements and how it should look. Have we ever wondered why? This is the place of worship and sacrifice, the place every Jew would visit with reverence as it is the place where God said He stays amongst His people. The very elaborate descriptions and plan of the building symbolises how the Lord wants His church to be.... The impression is that it is the Lord who is saying He determines how the building must look and likewise how the spiritual house must look and operate!!! He decides, not man!!

Eph 4:11 And He gave some as apostles, and some as prophets, and some as evangelists, and some as pastors and teachers, 12 for the equipping of the saints for the work of service, to the building up of the body of Christ; 13 until we all attain to the unity of the faith, and of the knowledge of the Son of God, to a mature man, to the measure of the stature which belongs to the fullness of Christ.

God Himself gave these gifts (not a title) for the equipping of each member so that they may grow into mature Christians which must become like Him (the fullness of Christ)!!!

1Co 12:14 For the body is not one member, but many. 15 If the foot should say, "Because I am not a hand, I am not a part of the body," it is not for this reason any the less a part of the body. 16 And if the ear should say, "Because I am not an eye, I am not a part of the body," it is not for this reason any the less a part of the body.
17 If the whole body were an eye, where would the hearing be? If the whole were hearing, where would the sense of smell be? 18.

But now God has placed the members, each one of them, in the body, just as He desired.

We must ask ourselves where these gifted appointees are. Who is assisting the pastor or apostle? (There are many explanations as to who and what an apostle is but I believe an apostle is a church planter with all the gifts of a teacher, prophet and healer, etc. An apostle has no individual church but a number of churches who supports his ministry. He may stay at a specific congregation for a time but will move on eventually).

1Co 12:28 And God has appointed in the church, first apostles, second prophets, third teachers, then miracles, then gifts of healings, helps, administrations, various kinds of tongues 29 All are not apostles, are they? All are not prophets, are they? All are not teachers, are they? All are not workers of miracles, are they?

We as followers and disciples of the Lord should often take stock of our situation and condition and judge whether we are in line with His revealed will and are still walking in the Spirit (true to our Lord's request that we walk according to the Spirit). Has anything crept in that we should take note of? Are the various gifts operating on our ministry? Has our ministry taken the place of our own personal worship and love for Him? Are we so "in control" that no space is given to the Lord. Is His will of so much less importance that we allow His voice to be drowned in our own self-willed zeal for the Lord, doing and structuring the church the way we decided He wants?

Cain made that same mistake, deciding for himself (self-will) how and what would please God and thereby sinned greatly! Abel, his brother, was following the Lord's commandment and offered up flesh and blood. Cain worked up a pride and refused to request the necessary from his brother. This pride culminated in a killing! I want to say this right here, that the Lord said the following which no church that I know of, has done fully: Mat_21:13 And He *said to them, "It is written, 'MY HOUSE SHALL BE CALLED A

HOUSE OF PRAYER'; but you are making it a ROBBERS' DEN." These words are taken up in 3 of the four gospels, emphasising their importance, yet we place prayer in second or third place? This is perhaps one example of what has gone wrong with our churches in general.

From Revelation 2 and 3 it is very clear that many evil things have crept into the church. The internationally known lecturer and writer of "Occult Invasion" (of the church), Dave Hunt, (ISBN 1-56507-831-4 dated 3 April 2005) makes it clear that Satan hates the church and has begun an internal strategy to make it of no effect. A subtle invasion is what he (Dave Hunt) refers to rather than a frontal attack, which of course would be easily recognised. Satan knows very well that the Lord said (just the same as when he knew what the Lord said to Adam) that if the "angels of the Lord" do not listen, their "lampstands" will be removed from them!! (Rev. 2 verse 5)

William L Ford, the writer of "Created for Influence", wrote, and I quote:

The stench is unbelievable. You quickly cover your mouth and nose. But it is still hard not to stare. The slab that was once an inviting pink colour is now a slimy grey, crawling with maggots and buzzing with flies. You feel like throwing it in a garbage can but then rather just get away as quickly as possible. Yuck!

Maybe you have never encountered a piece of rotten meat left to the elements for days on end. But this disgusting spectacle exactly describes the spiritual state of a culture when the church does not fulfil its role to be the "salt of the earth" (Matt. 5 verse 13).

I hope, pray and believe that this "book" will stir up a new hunger for the church amongst us to become relevant again, salt of the earth!

In a certain church in Stellenbosch South Africa the pastor would preach and then wait on Holy Spirit to further show what He wanted to do....the word was allowed to continue and manifest in hearts and minds with stunning results. Many testimonies and healings took place.

Love is action, not just words. Love is powerful, not just a feeling! Where has it gone? Young people who love the Lord have no problem with this. Why do we adults have a problem with it? The Holy Spirit can do far more than man and can bring about revival in hearts and minds. We need to become childlike in our faith!

Seeking God's will for our lives must precede the seeking of His will for the flock under our care. Think of His will as that which He will work in us as we yield in faith to His working in us and then through us. Matthew 9 verse 29 says *According to your faith be it unto you.* Andrew Murray states: *The stronger and more unceasing and joyfully confident your faith in God's working all His will in you becomes, the more you will know that it is possible for you to do that will.* (Gods Will Our Dwelling Place – Andrew Murray).

The word of the Lord says in Eph. 5 verse 15: *be careful how you walk...*and later: *...so then do not be foolish but understand what the will of God is.* Eph. 5 verse 10 by implication reveals that it will be a process in our lives: *...trying to learn what is pleasing to the Lord.* By trying we will already please Him and I believe blessings will follow him or her who tries!!!

A friend of mine once had a very urgent message for his pastor and went to his house on a Saturday to convey the message but his wife, who met him at the door said that Pastor N is in his study and she does not disturb him then.

My friend said his message is urgent whereupon she replied that he can go in but she dare not disturb him. My friend opened the study door slowly and peeping in he saw his pastor lying on his face, arms outstretched before the Lord in preparation for the Sunday service and decided to depart quietly.

Let us pray urgently for a fresh baptism of Holy Spirit in order to walk by faith and in the power of the Holy Spirit.

PREPARING OUR HEARTS

For us to receive this message fully there are three aspects we need to deal with, as sensitively but thoroughly as we can. These may well hinder or enhance the message's impact on our hearts; i.e. 1. Hunger for the truth, 2. The truth versus the false and then 3. The devastating effect of pride.

HUNGER FOR THE TRUTH

Copied from the Internet: Nancy Taylor Warner:

Recently, as I was in prayer for a need that had been shared with me, I thought I knew how to pray: I was familiar with all the scriptures relating to that need, so I would just begin to pray them! Much to my surprise, as I began to get quiet before the Lord, He led me in a whole new direction. Scripture after scripture came before me, as my prayer time turned into a prayerful little Bible study.

As I thought on the significance of the words that the Holy Spirit was quickening, I began to realize how essential it is <u>that we have a "present word" from the Lord</u>. Whether praying or speaking, we need to hear from the Lord, in order to speak forth His word, quickened and anointed, that His Spirit and life might flow through us.

Had I not heard from the Lord, I might have done a lot of praying, but I would have missed what was necessary to unlock the door for living faith to enter. How easy it is to miss! We can spend a lot of time that may not be fruitful time, even in our religious endeavours. How dependent we are on the Holy Spirit for accomplishing anything of Kingdom value!

How do we come up into a higher level of spiritually hearing from the Lord?

The enlargement of our spiritual capacity begins and **continues to grow through spiritual hunger,** *as I simply become awakened to the love song of the Lord and begin to respond.*

My dear brother and sister, the above shared experience underscores what I believe we need to do, that is, to allow ourselves to become hungry again, fire from on high!!

THE FALSE AND THE TRUE

Many are the people who heard that there are false prophets and indeed there are many. However there are also false apostles, witnesses and Christians:

2Co_11:13 For such men are false apostles, deceitful workers, disguising themselves as apostles of Christ.

2Co_11:26 I have been on frequent journeys, in dangers from rivers, dangers from robbers, dangers from my countrymen, dangers from the Gentiles, dangers in the city, dangers in the wilderness, dangers on the sea, dangers among false brethren;

Rev_2:2 'I know your deeds and your toil and perseverance, and that you cannot endure evil men, and you put to the test those who call themselves apostles, and they are not, and you found them to be false;

The English dictionary gives a couple of meanings of the word false:

1. *Not true or correct; erroneous: a false statement. 2. Uttering or declaring what is untrue: a false witness. 3. Not*

faithful or loyal; treacherous: a false friend. 4. Tending to deceive or mislead; deceptive: a false impression. 5. Not genuine; counterfeit. 6. Based on mistaken, erroneous, or inconsistent impressions, ideas, or facts: false pride. 7. Used as a substitute or supplement, especially temporarily: false supports for a bridge. 8. Not properly, accurately, or honestly made, done, or adjusted: a false balance. 9. Inaccurate in pitch, as a musical note.

Of the above explanations I found that of the above the following would perhaps be more relevant to the false ministers or ministries:

5. Not genuine; counterfeit.
6. Based on mistaken, erroneous, or inconsistent impressions, ideas, or facts.
9. Inaccurate in pitch, as a musical note.

PRIDE COMES BEFORE THE FALL

It would seem that pride causes much of this "falseness". I believe most started off right but somewhere got lost? Pride comes before the fall? Jas_4:6

But He gives a greater grace. Therefore it says, "GOD IS OPPOSED TO THE PROUD, BUT GIVES GRACE TO THE HUMBLE."

In the dictionary the word "pride" is described as follows:
A feeling of deep pleasure or satisfaction derived from one's own achievements, the achievements of one's close associates, or from qualities or possessions that are widely admired.

Can the reader see what I see here: <u>*derived from one's own achievements*</u> and: *from qualities or possessions that are <u>widely admired</u>.* The most dangerous opinion to have of the work we do for the Lord is that it is us, our abilities and goodness!!

Another dictionary explains pride like this: *the quality of being worthy of esteem or respect. self-esteem, self-**pride**. a feeling of*

***pride** in yourself. Ego, egotism,* self-importance. *An inflated feeling of **pride** in your superiority to others*

Pride is at the very top of the list of things God hates. "These six things doth the Lord hate: yea, seven are an abomination unto him: a proud look, (Proverbs 6:16-19).

King Saul's whole life is an example of how his lack of faith in God led him to pride and his own demise. When Samuel confronts Saul about this disobedience, Saul's pride leaps into action to cover up the real issue. The first thing he does is blame Samuel: *"because he did not come within the days appointed"*

He does admit that he was worried about the people who were leaving him but claims that if Samuel just would have shown up on time this would have never happened and makes himself appear as the victim. Pride will convince us that it is in our best interest to make ourselves the victim through blame when confronted with our own moral failures.

A testimony from the Internet (By David Wilkerson February 8, 1988) explains pride very well:

God sees pride in an entirely different way than we do. He showed me that I had too narrow a definition of pride. Yes, there is a wicked, boastful, arrogant pride, and it can be seen all about us in these days. But there is also a pride that is spiritual in nature. It is committed by those who have walked closely with God and it can be seen in the holiest among us. <u>The more spiritual you are, the more revelation you have had, the closer to Him that you have been, the more hideous this sin is when it is committed. It is not a way of life, although it could become so. It is a sin that is often committed even on our knees, while seeking God.</u>

To understand this message, I want to give you new definitions of pride and humility. Pride is independence - humility is dependence. Pride is an unwillingness to wait for God to act in His own time and in His own way.

Pride rushes in to take matters into its own hands. One of the greatest temptations true Christians face is getting ahead of God. It is acting without a clear mandate from God. It is taking things into our own hands when it appears that God is not working fast enough. It is impatience
As soon as King Saul took matters into his own hands, Samuel arrived. Divine direction was right at the door, just minutes away! But Saul couldn't wait!

"And is shall be said in that day, Lo this is our God; we have waited for him, and he will save us; this is the Lord, we have waited for him we will be glad and rejoice in his Salvation..." (Isaiah 25:9).

"For since the beginning of the world men have not heard, nor perceived by the ear, neither hath the eye seen, O God, beside thee, what he hath prepared for him that <u>waiteth</u> for him... (Isaiah 64:4).

Pride is repelled by the idea of servanthood. Today everybody wants to be everything but a servant. We quote this Scripture, "Thou art no more a servant, but a son; and if a son, then an heir of God through Christ" (Galatians 4:7). What Paul is really saying is that a son who has been tutored correctly knows that he is legally the king's son with all rights, but he so loves his father he chooses the role of a servant. Paul in the same book said he was "a servant of Jesus Christ" (Roman 1: 1), James called himself "a servant of the Lord Jesus" (2 Peter 1:1). And Christ, the Lord, the very Son of God "made himself of no reputation, and took upon Him the form of a servant, and was made in the likeness of men .... He humbled Himself and became obedient unto death, even the death of the cross" (Philippians 2:7-8), Let this mind be in you, which was also in Christ Jesus. A servant has no will of his own; his master's word is his will.

The Cross Represents the death of all my own plans, all my own ideas, my own desires, my own hopes and dreams. It is most of all the absolute death of my own will. This is true humility. Humility is associated only with the Cross. "He humbled Himself and became obedient unto death at the cross. (Philippians 2:7-8). He had told His disciples,

<u>It is when you go down into the grave of death to all self, all ambition, all self-will, that you hear His voice.</u> Jesus said, "The hour is coming, and now is, when the dead shall hear the voice of the Son of God... All that are in the graves shall hear His voice" (John 5:25, 28), this is why thousands of Christians today are getting into trouble hearing still small voices. There is confusion, things are not coming out right, because there has been no dying to self-will. Yes, I believe God does speak to His children. You can hear His true, holy, unmistakable voice, <u>but only after crucifixion of self-will and self-desire.</u> Jesus heard clearly from the Father. So did Paul, Peter, John and Stephen; but only because they were dead to this world. They were consumed with doing His will only.

(Copyright © 2002 by World Challenge, Lindale Texas USA).

Being too impressed with the result of God's word.

All of us will encounter the problem of being honoured by men for what we accomplish in the spirit and then feeling soooo good about it. When this occurs many times and frequently, our self-esteem rises above normal and we feel important. Jesus new this could happen and explained it thus:

Matt. 23 verse 5 onwards:

But all their works they do for to be seen of men: they make broad their phylacteries, and enlarge the borders of their garments, :6 And love the uppermost rooms at feasts, and the chief seats in the synagogues,:7 And greetings in the markets, and to be called of men, Rabbi, Rabbi. 8 But be not ye called Rabbi: for one is your Master, even Christ; and all ye are brethren.:9 And call no man your father upon the earth: for one is your Father, which is in heaven.:10 Neither be ye called masters: for one is your Master, even Christ. 11 But he that is greatest among you shall be your servant.

In John 5 verse 44 we read:

How can ye believe, which receive honour one of another, and seek not the honour that cometh from God only?

From God <u>ONLY</u>

Significant of the above is the fact that Jesus says...be not ye be called..... We must ensure that we are not lifted high!! Do not be called Rabbi, Apostle, Prophet, Pastor or Father!!! How do you prevent this? When Paul refers to himself as apostle he is referring to his calling and office, not his title. He was just Paul to his fellow Christians. He saw himself as the chief sinner! Jesus is clearly admonishing us to ensure we are seen as "servants", known as "servants" and stay humble in being called John or Peter, or Paul.

This is a difficult subject to deal with but I will endeavour to explain what I heard the Lord say about this aspect of ministry. We all have to work with God`s word, preach it and teach it. God`s word is powerful and beautiful at the same time! It is a fragrance leading to life!! The Logos and Rhema word of God is knowledge which ultimately leads to salvation. God`s word is powerful and very effective. We know this by experience. (You shall know the truth and the truth shall set you free).

God`s word is actually the Word that has become flesh amongst us: (Joh 1:14 And the Word was made flesh, and dwelt among us, *and we beheld his glory, the glory as of the only begotten of the Father, full of grace and truth.*) Furthermore in John 1 verse 1 we read that the Word was God: *In the beginning was the Word, and the Word was with God, and the Word was God.*) Can you now understand why the Lord is standing amongst the lampstands with "burning" eyes: Rev 1:14 His head and *his* hairs *were* white like wool, as white as snow; and his eyes *were* as a flame of fire; We are to deal very carefully with God`s Word!!

What may happen to us leaders as we preach (use) the word of God we can become so impressed by His word, by the reactions of man (praises of man) and own emotions that the One who uttered them comes second!!

The greatest danger for us leaders is to want to keep the glory for ourselves. Men and women can be very convincing and flattering. We may forget that what we experience is God, is heaven come down! Over many years we succumb to this type of "worship" and do not realise the danger of not always giving or returning to Him the glory.

One day I ministered to senior staff members after I prayed for success and having been congratulated and thanked, I drove back home feeling "on top" just so "happy" and good but suddenly I realised oops, I have taken the glory for me. Whilst still driving I asked forgiveness and gave it to Him by lifting the "feeling" to Him. Wow, immediately the feeling was gone completely, so fast that I felt to at least take some back but then I realised again, the flesh wants to be recognised and I just gave everything to Him. Then peace came down, just a knowledge that He was happy and I received a teaching from Him personally, wow!!

Yet I know this danger lurks forever and I need to watch my heart.

Our Lord set a little child before the disciples, solemnly assuring them, that unless they were converted and made like little children, they could not enter his kingdom. Children, when very young, do not desire authority, do not regard outward distinctions, are free from malice, are teachable, and willingly dependent on their parents. It is true that they soon begin to show other dispositions, and other ideas are taught them at an early age; but these are marks of childhood, and render them proper emblems of the lowly minds of true Christians. Surely we need to be daily renewed in the spirit of our minds that we may become simple and humble, as little children, and willing to be the least of all. Let us daily study this subject, and examine our own spirits.

JOHN AND THE ANGELS

John, who is the beloved disciple was the one whom the others would ask to speak to the Lord as he was so close to Jesus on earth. Our Lord chooses this disciple to speak to His angels the pastor/preacher/prophet/teacher in charge of His church!! It is a "love letter". The Lord is holy and pure and wants His Lampstands (all of them - 7) to be like pure gold!! He wants us, His pastor/preacher/prophet/teacher that is in charge of a church to be pure and holy, completely. He wants us to serve the church for Him, as Him and pure and holy like Him!! He holds us in His right hand!!! He uses us to purify the church, the lampstand, the gold!! How can we do this if we allow some evil things to enter the church? How can we do what He wants if we as an example have lost our first love (Rev. 2 verse 5)!! We have chosen to "escape" from His right hand?

He who has an ear, let him hear what the Spirit is saying to the churches (7). We have been dodging this message as if it is sent to thousands or millions of church members. No, members are not able to rectify a church by themselves...it is impossible...YOU AND I, my dear pastor/preacher/prophet/teacher in charge of His church, You and I are addressed here and YOU and I are responsible!! You and I are also capable, a star, if we stay in His hand!!!

Our Lord is holding US in His right hand standing amongst the GOLDEN Lampstands and with His eyes like fire are looking at the lampstands and then commands John the beloved disciple to write what He wants to say to US the angels (pastor/preacher/teacher, etc.) of the Golden lampstand churches' the stars in His hand.

His (Jesus) stars, angels, pastor/preacher/prophet/teacher are the key to purifying the golden lampstands, the churches!! We must choose to do what the Word of God is asking of us, even now!!

In fact it is as if the Lord is saying to John, "tell My angel at Ephesus....!! Tell My pastor, preacher, teacher, prophet at Ephesus, at Hermanus, Mossel Bay, Bellville, New York, etc. You all are in My hand and must choose again to serve Me and Me only. We are to correct the church, the lampstand of gold!! We are stars in His hand, we are capable, and we must choose....and He says: repent and do the deeds you did at first (maybe before we were influenced by fame, members, money, power, etc.).

GOLDEN LAMPSTANDS

In Rev. 1 verse 12 and 13 we see Jesus portrayed as standing in the middle of seven golden lampstands. Jesus our Lord does not here have us guess what is meant by these as it is explained in verse 20....these represent the churches!!!! What is also significant here is that lampstands have no use unless they are fed with oil that brings forth light. Without oil there will be no true light.

Lampstands representing the churches! These lampstands are very significant and full of prophetic meaning. The 7 branches or lamps of each lampstand represent the seven Spirits of Revelation (Holy Spirit) and indicates fullness or completeness. The Lord equips each church with the necessary spiritual attributes to be the Bride of Christ and they are: (Isa 11.....

- The Spirit of the Lord
- The Spirit of wisdom
- The Spirit of understanding
- The Spirit of council
- The Spirit of strength
- The Spirit of knowledge
- The Spirit of the fear of the Lord

As leader of the flock we are specifically empowered by the Spirit of the Lord to know the Lord and know His will, be full of wisdom, knowledge and understanding, able to council and walk in the fear (carefully and prayerfully) of the Lord in strength (bold and unflinching).

In many ways, the tabernacle in the wilderness was typical of the Lord's church today. The tabernacle was built under the direction of God. God gave the pattern to Moses and told him: Ex. 25:8 "And let them make me a sanctuary; that I may dwell among them. 9 According to all that I show thee, after the pattern of the tabernacle, and the pattern of all the instruments thereof, even so shall ye make it." Truly God was the King giving direction to the children of Israel and they were to follow those directions. <u>They were not to deviate from them.</u>

Likewise, Christ, the King, is the builder of His church: Mat. 16:18 *"And I say also unto thee, that thou art Peter, and upon this rock (Jesus) I will build my church; and the gates of hell shall not prevail against it."* This verse should be coupled with Ps. 127:1 *"Except the LORD build the house, they labour in vain that build it: except the LORD keep the city, the watchman waketh but in vain."* This teaches us that our King Jesus gives us directions and a pattern for His house (church).

We are to follow the directions and pattern he has given us for the building and worship of and in His house. We are not to deviate from it. When the Lord instructs us that He wants His house to be a house of prayer He literally means just that! The main thing they should be doing is pray!!! Prayer can take on many forms, even worship, but pray we must.

Gold in scripture also signifies endurance, purity and able to withstand fire, which is precisely the way our ministry in the church should be. A person's work should be able to withstand the fire; a person's life should be able to be refined like gold. His church is also to be refined like gold. Reading chapters 2 and 3 it seems that the churches require refining to become totally pure?

There are many issues Jesus is not satisfied with, some very serious.

1 Cor 3 verses 12 to 14: Now if anyone builds on this foundation with gold, silver, precious stones, wood, hay, straw, each one's work will become clear; for the Day will declare is, because it will be revealed by fire; and the fire will test each one's work, of what sort it is. If anyone's work which he has built on it endures, he will receive a reward."–

My dear pastor, preacher, teacher, prophet, evangelist, leader, you are in the right hand of the Lord and He expects you to ensure that His lampstands are pure!! Pure gold!! Each person should be on the road to his or her "full purpose" in the Lord. They should know their gifts and how they operate in the body of Christ. They should also understand how their gifting assists in their witnessing to the lost.

The Apostle Paul is saying that all Christians will be tested *<u>when they leave this world</u>. Their works, or what kind of ministry they did while here, will go through the fire—if it is weak things like hay or straw, it will not endure. If it is gold, however, it stands a likely chance of enduring. It was work that was eternal and meaningful. After all, gold is refined by fire (<u>Rev. 3:18</u>), not destroyed.

Personally I believe that the refining is not only one Day but in fact now, daily, as well!! Our works are tested daily....the enemy is hard at work to destroy what we build in the spirit and we know it will only stand if it is from the Lord. For example: If we win someone to the Lord and he or she falls away, our work was not complete and maybe faulty!!

Reading Revelation chapter 1 verse 14 I see the Lords eyes like fire as in 1 Cor 3 :13 *Every man's work shall be made manifest: for the day shall declare it, because it shall be revealed by fire; and the fire shall try every man's work of what sort it is.* The Lord is adamant that His "angels" be pure and holy and obedient. They should hear Him, love Him and follow Him at all cost!! They must tend and serve the Bride of Christ as Christ would if He was here in the flesh!!!! But we are in the flesh and are His home, His abode, His temple! We are the carriers of His will and His heart!!

We are to follow the directions and pattern he has given us for the building and worship of and in His house. We are not to deviate from it. When the Lord instructs us that He wants His house to be a house of prayer He literally means just that!

Chris Hamman

THE CHURCH

The book of Revelation refers to lampstands (menorah) seven times in six verses (Rev. 1:12, 13, 20; 2:1, 5; and 11:4). The apostle John tells us that he saw the lampstands for the first time after he turned to see who was speaking to him. In the tabernacle during Israel's journey through the desert, the lampstand provided light for the High Priest to minister before the Lord. Likewise the Holy Spirit today provides light to understand scripture (The Word of God) and how to minister to the Lord.

In Rev. 1 verse 20 we see the meaning of these lampstands, 7 of them!! :

"As for the mystery of the seven stars which you saw in My right hand, and the seven golden lampstands: the seven stars are the angels of the seven churches, and the seven lampstands **are the seven churches.**

Without the Holy Spirit being in control of the church, it will ultimately lose its flavour, its shine, its light and God says: Rev 2:5 *'Remember therefore from where you have fallen, and repent and do the deeds you did at first; or else I am coming to you, and will remove your lampstand out of its place--unless you repent.*

When Israel sinned, the temple is destroyed and the lampstand removed:

The Book of Maccabees records that Antiochus Epiphanes took away the lampstands (plural) when he invaded and robbed the Temple (1 Maccabees 1:21). The later record of the making of "new holy vessels" may refer to the manufacture of new lampstands (1 Maccabees 4:49). There is no biblical mention of the fate of the menorah.

The fate of the menorah used in the Second Temple is recorded by Josephus, who states that it was brought to Rome and carried along during the triumph of Vespasian and Titus. The menorah was deposited afterwards in the Temple of Peace in Rome

Rev 2:5 'Remember therefore from where you have fallen, and repent and do the deeds you did at first; or else I am coming to you, and will remove your lampstand out of its place--unless you repent.

For the Lord's stars or angels to stay in His right hand they need to walk by the Spirit. "Rom 8 v 8 Those who are in the flesh (walking in the flesh) cannot please God...." Verse 13 states: *If you are living according to the flesh (e.g. human reasoning, etc.) you MUST die....!!* Listen to Paul as he states in Rom 1 verse 9...*whom I serve in the spirit*...." (Not in the flesh). The Lord Himself is in the midst of His church (where two or three gather in My name there I will be in their midst!!!) The Lord asks of you and me to walk in the spirit, not in the flesh!!

The oil (Spirit of God)

Zechariah 4 says that there are two olive trees beside the golden lampstand. The prophet Zechariah asked, "What are these, sir?" (v. 4). The angel answered, "Not by might nor by power, **but by My Spirit**, says Jehovah of hosts" (v. 6). Here, therefore, the revelation of the Spirit is implied. It is not until Zechariah 4 that there is a revelation—**a revelation concerning the Spirit.**

The church is a golden candlestick, or lamp-bearer, set up for enlightening this dark world, and holding forth the light of Divine revelation. Two olive trees were seen, one on each side the candlestick, from which oil flowed into the bowl without ceasing. Without going into detail about the two trees, what is evident is that the lampstand is fed by them, they are olive trees and oil is supplied for the lampstand to shine, to give light!! (Zechariah 4 verse 3) In the tabernacle Moses built the lamps of the menorah were lit daily from fresh, consecrated olive oil and burned from evening until morning, according to Exodus 27:21. The priest had to do this daily. Here the inference is that the lampstand is fed, daily, without human intervention. "Not by might nor by power, **but by My Spirit,**

The lamps were filled daily to keep them burning, depicting we the church (and us individually) need a fresh inpouring of the Holy Spirit daily. The same symbolism is used when the Israelites had to harvest the manna every day because it went bad and could not be used the next day. You and I, my dear and revered pastor, preacher, teacher, etc. need a daily filling…fresh oil!!

Someone said once: If God does not show up at your meeting, that meeting is of no consequence. Without the Holy Spirit the church has no role to play, no light to shine, no victory to proclaim.

Joh 16:7 "But I tell you the truth, it is to your advantage that I go away; for if I do not go away, the Helper (Holy Spirit) shall not come to you; but if I go, I will send Him to you.

Mat 25:1 "Then the kingdom of heaven will be comparable to ten virgins, who took their lamps, and went out to meet the bridegroom. Mat 25:8 "And the foolish said to the prudent, 'Give us some of your **oil**, for our lamps are going out. Without the Oil the Lampstand is ineffective and not able to function, that is to give LIGHT!!! The church will not be able to shine in this dark world we live in where Satan rules at the moment. It will succumb to the world and become like it!! Many churches have abandoned the teaching of the Holy Spirit and have given birth to dead followers.

The Spirit of God

Rev 1:4 John to the seven churches that are in Asia: Grace to you and peace, from Him who is and who was and who is to come; and **from the seven Spirits who are before His throne;**

Rev_3:1 "And to the angel of the church in Sardis write: He who has the **seven Spirits of God,** and the seven stars, says this: 'I know your deeds, that you have a name that you are alive, but you are dead.

Isa 11:2 *And the Spirit of the LORD will rest on Him, The Spirit of wisdom and understanding, The Spirit of counsel and strength, The Spirit of knowledge and the fear of the LORD.*

Isa 11:3 *And He will delight in the fear of the LORD, And <u>He will not judge by what His eyes see, Nor make a decision by what His ears hear;</u>*

Isa 11:4 *But with righteousness He will judge the poor, And decide with fairness for the afflicted of the earth; And He will strike the earth with the rod of His mouth, And with the breath of His lips He will slay the wicked.*

- The Spirit of the Lord
- The Spirit of wisdom
- The Spirit of understanding
- The Spirit of council
- The Spirit of strength
- The Spirit of knowledge
- The Spirit of the fear of the Lord

<u>He will not judge by what His eyes see, nor make a decision by what His ears hear.</u>

"Not by might nor by power, <u>but by My Spirit,</u> says Jehovah of hosts"

This Lampstand must have fresh oil (the 7 Spirits) daily and must not make a decision by what their ears hear not their eyes see. (Not be influenced by the world or men)

Now consider the spiritual **lack of the "stars, angels"** of the churches as mentioned in Revelation 2 and 3:

Rev 2:4 'But I have this against you, that you have left your first love.
Rev 2:10 'Do not fear what you are about to suffer.
Rev 2:14 'But I have a few things against you, because you have there some who hold the teaching of Balaam, who kept teaching Balak to put a stumbling block before the sons of Israel, to eat things sacrificed to idols, and to commit *acts of* immorality.

Rev 2:15 'Thus you also have some who in the same way hold the teaching of the Nicolaitans.

Rev 2:20 'But I have *this* against you, that you tolerate the woman Jezebel, who calls herself a prophetess, and she teaches and leads My bond-servants astray, so that they commit *acts of* immorality and eat things sacrificed to idols.
Rev 3:1 "And to the angel of the church in Sardis write: He who has the seven Spirits of God, and the seven stars, says this: 'I know your deeds, that you have a name that you are alive, but you are dead.

Rev 3:11 'I am coming quickly; hold fast what you have, in order that no one take your crown.

The Holy Spirit who convicts us of sin is clearly not being followed in every instance. Each of the 7 branches of the Lampstand had to be given fresh Oil. Knowledge and Understanding, Wisdom and the Fear of the Lord, Council and Strength and what is more, each "star" must reaslise that:

Mat 18:20 "For where two or three have gathered together in My name, there I am in their midst."

The very first of the seven Spirits mentioned in Isaiah 11 verse 2 is: And the Spirit of the LORD......

Maybe many churches have become more like an organisation and run like a business? The word is preached there and then the members must go and do. The Word of God is dissected and interpreted by the flesh, not the Spirit, who is the author thereof!

Luk 19:46 saying to them, "It is written, 'AND MY HOUSE SHALL BE A HOUSE OF PRAYER,' but you have made it a ROBBERS' DEN.

This is just about the last function considered important today and many pastors, etc. are not willing to give it pre-eminence!! Missionary work is likewise seen as just a part of the churches function. Expanding the Kingdom and looking after the poor and needy is the main purpose of the church, after worshipping Him in spirit and in truth.

Mat 18:12 "What do you think? If any man has a hundred sheep, and one of them has gone astray, does he not leave the ninety-nine on the mountains and go and search for the one that is straying?
Mat 18:13 "And if it turns out that he finds it, truly I say to you, he rejoices over it more than over the ninety-nine which have not gone astray.
Mat 18:14 "Thus it is not *the* will of your Father who is in heaven that one of these little ones perish.

Do we realize "little one" refer to also an adult! I have ministered to many such individuals who the verses in Matthew refer to: Mat 5:3 Blessed *are* the poor in spirit: for theirs is the kingdom of heaven. The Lord was cross with Israel for they did not look after or care for the poor and the widow!! In some charismatic churches I found they minister very effectively to such individuals under the guidance of the Holy Spirit and become involved physically with the needs of them being ministered to! It is not all hype and sound but true love for each member. I found prayer to be a strong emphasis with such churches, even during the service, groups were praying for the word to be effective and bring in the lost, heal and minister to the needy, etc. Manifestations of the Holy Spirit is an integral part of the service but not sought consciously. He blows where He wills

One of the problems many spiritual leaders face is that they cannot discern if a manifestation of the Holy Spirit is in fact just that or false. The easiest way out for them is to see it all as false. Manifestations of the Spirit is such an awesome "tool" in the hands of the Lord (healing, joy, sorrow, provision) that our enemy has tried to negate its need and power, its worth and truth.

Satan cannot create anything. He is himself a created being. All he can do is copy, so that is exactly what he does, even to healing people!! Revelations clearly states that this is possible (Rev 13 v 12)!! He copies manifestations of laughter, joy, falling under the spirit. He even copies mourning and sadness!! I saw this with my own eyes on the mission field, crying and mourning that was pure flesh and not deep down sorrow!! So religion without the Spirit of God, without power (2 Ti 3 v 5) is the result.

There are many evangelists, especially Telly-evangelists who ride on the popularity of signs and wonders resulting in the praises of men and have become caricatures of the real thing!! They stomp and rave, shout and wave the handkerchief or the bible! They use the microphone and ask members being ministered too to say what is happening, etc. I found many of these evangelists sadly hungry for attention and seem to be lacking in agape love!! Please do not let these stop you from seeking the Holy Spirit in your ministry.

There is a tendency amongst some spiritual leaders in discrediting others. Some sought to discredit the preachers with statements they made that may be unbiblical and some were criticized for visiting the Pope, etc. Some are criticised for their "unbiblical style of preaching"! This activity draws our focus away from our own lack and needs. I have tried to explain in the above paragraphs what is required from the stars, God`s "stars" the angels of the 7 churches.

None of us can attain to the standard of holiness God requires on our own, we need the Holy Spirit: Joh 16:13 Howbeit *when he, the Spirit of truth, is come, he will guide you into all truth: for he shall not speak of himself; but whatsoever he shall hear, that shall he speak: and he will shew you things to come!!*

Congregation/church

In the New Testament it is the translation of the Greek word ecclesia, which is synonymous with the Hebrew kahal of the Old Testament, both words meaning simply an assembly, the character of which can only be known from the connection in which the word is found. (Copied from the internet: http://www.biblestudytools.com/dictionary/church/ :)

We find the word ecclesia used in the following senses in the New Testament:

1. *It is translated "assembly" in the ordinary classical sense (Acts 19:32 Acts 19:39 Acts 19:41).*

2. *It denotes the whole body of the redeemed, all those whom the Father has given to Christ, the invisible catholic church (Ephesians 5:23 Ephesians 5:25 Ephesians 5:27 Ephesians 5:29 ; Hebrews 12:23).*

3. *A few Christians associated together in observing the ordinances of the gospel are an ecclesia (Romans 16:5 ; Colossians 4:15).*

4. *All the Christians in a particular city, whether they assembled together in one place or in several places for religious worship, were an ecclesia. Thus all the disciples in Antioch, forming several congregations, were one church (Acts 13:1); so also we read of the "church of God at Corinth" (1 Corinthians 1:2), "the church at Jerusalem" (Acts 8:1), "the church of Ephesus" (Revelation 2:1), etc.*

5. *The whole body of professing Christians throughout the world (1 Corinthians 15:9 ; Galatians 1:13 ; Matthew*

16:18) are the church of Christ. The church visible "consists of all those throughout the world that profess the true religion, together with their children." It is called "visible" because its members are known and its assemblies are public.

Considering the truth of the above, that the word church basically refers to the coming together of the children of God in one place, this promise of the Lord comes to mind: "*Where two or three gather in My name there I am in their midst*" (Mat_18:20)! The ark or presence of the Lord being in heaven according to Rev. 11 verse 19 denotes the fact that God is no longer "contained" in a building but in the people. He now lives in us as we "enter" heaven itself. *Mar_10:15 "Truly I say to you, whoever does not receive the kingdom of God like a child shall not enter it at all." Mar_12:34 And when Jesus saw that he had answered intelligently, He said to him, "You are not far from the kingdom of God." And after that, no one would venture to ask Him any more questions.*

Luk_10:9 and heal those in it who are sick, and say to them, 'The kingdom of God has come near to you.'

It seems we have made the church an "authority" whereas it actually denotes the congregation (coming together) of a group of followers of the Lord who have created some regulations and methods amongst themselves that order their coming together so that the common purpose is met effectively, i.e. worshipping God, experiencing His presence, and witnessing for the expansion of the Kingdom of God. For this purpose the Lord gave some essential gifts to the "group": i.e. pastors, evangelists, preachers and teachers as well as prophets. Please note these are not titles but a gifting, an office or a responsibility. As soon as we create levels of "authority" we lift man up instead of the Lord!

The Lord said "where two or three gather in My name....the "church" or tabernacle which is my body, becomes more than one and He then dwells amongst us, creating a unity of the spirit.

Church leaders must have this absolute truth in their minds and hearts, that Jesus is the centre of it all. No one else must be lifted high, only Him. Thinking that education and knowledge has placed us above someone else is a sin. Knowledge and education is essential and must not be ignored at all, but it should result in a greater understanding of servanthood, not rulership. The more we get to know Him, the more we get to understanding Him, the more we will esteem Him and our brothers and sisters in the Lord. The more we bow down, the more we will serve and the more we become sons of the living God. Teaching has its place yet the manifest presence of the Lord will accomplish so much more, so much faster!!

Without the Holy Spirit being in control of the church, it will ultimately lose its flavour, its shine, its light and God says: Rev 2:5 *'Remember therefore from where you have fallen, and repent and do the deeds you did at first; or else I am coming to you, and will remove your lampstand out of its place--unless you repent.*

The mystery the world seeks in all sorts of religions, mysticism, Buddhism, scientism, Catholicism, reincarnation, Muslim, congusianisim, etc. does not even come close to matching the mystery of Christ and God's Holy Spirit. The mystery that causes a Muslim royal prince to accept Jesus Christ in the face of death by the hands of his own family, a witchdoctor who renounces all and burns his wicket instruments of darkness, a Satanist who gets born again by the blood of the Lamb, an atheist who suddenly finds joy and peace in the Lord or a prisoner who lies prostrate before the cross of Calvary, is the greatest mystery off all. A man of violence turned into a man of peace and even a gentle giant, a beggar who obtains hope and a new life from Him, yes, miracles mysteriously unfolds before our very eyes, yet the world is blind and deaf.

God is preparing a table and we will take our place in His presence. Jesus accomplished all of this, all of it. Jesus the Lamb of God....did you hear? God's Lamb...It is His sacrifice...the only Son, the greatest mystery of all, our Redeemer.

Darkness will flee when we praise Him! How great Thou art!!!! This song is often chosen by secular artists due to its intense meaning...and often raise the roof in applause..... However, when it is sung from the heart of a believer it affects the atmosphere in heaven and angels join in to worship Him. How great Thou art!!!!

At rebirth we receive a new "wineskin" in which the "new wine" the Spirit of God, can be contained. Even to overflowing! Sometimes we cannot contain what is poured in by the Lord and we overflow in gratitude, love and song. We are often called to pray when we are consumed (overflow) by what the Spirit brings and then we start to minister on behalf of others. We then become the trumpet, the voice, the vessel of His choice as we flow in the Spirit of the Lord.

He again says to us, come, come and drink from the well of provision, come all who are thirsty, for more and more, especially for the sake of others, not self. Come and drink to overflowing for the healing of the nations...and make My bride ready for the table is laid and the invitations sent. The hour has come for the bride to be made ready. I have more than enough...do not be shy, come and drink. Your own heart needs this overflowing as well as those who you need to minister to also. Ask and I will not delay...for now is the time.

Chris Hamman

REVELATION 2 verse 1

Rev 2:1 "To the angel of the church in Ephesus write

Taking a closer look at the first letter (to Ephesus) I noted that this church leader was doing some good stuff. He made sure no false apostle (preacher) was allowed to minister (Rev. 2 verse 2). In 2 Co 11 we read: *13 For such men are false apostles, deceitful workers, disguising themselves as apostles of Christ. 4 And no wonder, for even Satan disguises himself as an angel of light. 15 Therefore it is not surprising if his servants also disguise themselves as servants of righteousness; whose end shall be according to their deeds.*

This leader also protected the flock from evil men: Rev 2:2 *'I know your deeds and your toil and perseverance, and that you cannot endure evil men.* In 1 Co 5 we read: *1 It is actually reported that there is immorality among you, and immorality of such a kind as does not exist even among the Gentiles, that someone has his father's wife. 2 And you have become arrogant, and have not mourned instead, in order that the one who had done this deed might be removed from your midst.*

I would admire such a one who does not fear to minister in great authority and power! Yet the Lord is not satisfied as this one lost his love for the Lord, his first love! The good stuff is done in self-righteousness? To Israel the Lord said: Isa 1:11 *"What are your multiplied sacrifices to Me?" Says the LORD. "I have had enough of burnt offerings of rams, And the fat of fed cattle. And I take no pleasure in the blood of bulls, lambs, or goats. 12 "When you come to appear before Me, Who requires of you this trampling of My courts?*

This trespass of lost love is so devastating that it will result in the lampstand being removed. The Lord is saying "I have had enough of this lovelessness"? Doing things for the Lord without love is a sort of churchy thing we do...we have programs that depict when and how we must conduct a service? I have often wondered whether pastors who repeat certain religious statements Sunday after Sunday really still mean what they say from the heart. "I have to preach, I have to allow singing, I have to pray at certain times, etc. Even though we realise it has no fruit we continue, Sunday after Sunday.

One Sunday-morning I attended the second service of a church I frequented and noted the sort of sad faces of 99% of the congregation leaving the first service. I asked the pastor why and he said you cannot judge by men's faces!!!

Gen_4:6 Then the LORD said to Cain, "Why are you angry? And why has your countenance fallen?

Job_9:27 "Though I say, 'I will forget my complaint, I will leave off my sad countenance and be cheerful,'

Psa_10:4 The wicked, in the haughtiness of his countenance, does not seek Him. All his thoughts are, "There is no God."

Psa_42:11 Why are you in despair, O my soul? And why have you become disturbed within me? Hope in God, for I shall yet praise Him, The help of my countenance, and my God.

The joy of the Lord? Where is it then? A celebration is a joyful event!! Always!! The Lord said where two or three gather in My name there I am in their midst!! Joy!! We experience His presence corporately, as a family!! Joy and happiness!! Love is never or rarely, sad!!

Rom 13:8 Owe nothing to anyone except to love one another; for he who loves his neighbor has fulfilled *the* law.

Understanding the Relationship

Psa. 26:8 O LORD, I love the habitation of Thy house, And the place where Thy glory dwells.

David wants to be with the Lord he loves...The Lord's presence was in the Temple or Sanctuary. He brought the Ark (The presence of the Lord) back from where it was left by the enemy and organised a 24/7 choir with instruments to sing before the Lord. He appointed people to keep the area clean and restored the position of the Levites.

Studying Rev 2 we see that the minister (star) is doing some things right:

Rev 2:2 'I know your deeds and your toil and perseverance, and that you cannot endure evil men, and you put to the test those who call themselves apostles, and they are not, and you found them *to be* false;
Rev 2:3 and you have perseverance and have endured for My name's sake, and have not grown weary.

Rev 2:4 "But I have this against you, that you have left your first love".

It is as if the Lord is saying that His ministers are doing some things which are pleasing but that the main thing is left behind, loving Him first. Putting all else second. When we pray, for example, our adoration and worship should automatically flow from our hearts first and not the issues of life or the ministry!! They come second!!

Once again, I want to return here to my previous reference to John who is the beloved disciple. He was the one whom the others would ask to speak to the Lord as he was so close to Jesus on earth.

Our Lord chooses this disciple to speak to His angels the pastor/preacher/prophet/teacher in charge of His church!! It is a "love letter".

Without love every gift and calling, every talent and spiritual strength becomes polluted and fleshly, worldly. "Thou shall Love thy God...." was not just a command, it was a life giving truth and principle set by God. Without godly love, agape love, the enemy can subtly enter the scene and bring his own lies. God is love, He does not just love, He is IT. It is His makeup, His character, His very self..... God is love!! So everything He does, decides or thinks rests in love. His Word is cast in love and to use His word you and I need to also love, love Him first, love our Neighbours and the poor and widows especially!!!. Gifts and callings are cast in love, outside of love it breeds death!! This is the truth!!

King David was so glad the Lord is again in their midst (The Ark returns) that he, the mighty King of Israel, the one the Philistines fear, dances so wildly, so without constraint, that his kingly gown lifts to expose his undies!!! His love for the Lord knew no bounds. This is a far cry from the sombre atmosphere in some churches today!! When we visit a church where the people worship with loud voices and gesticulating bodies, reflecting their exuberant gladness and joy, we feel uncomfortable and even criticise! David's wife also critisised the king and became barren as a result of her critical spirit.

If we lose our love, our first love for Him, our motivations, our reason for "working with Him" is replaced with the flesh, our minds, the council of fleshly people! We seek advice from men and not from Him. We even seek and react to man's love and admiration. Fact is we lose the ability to hear Him!! We work for a salary and a financially rewarding job! We work for the praises of people and judge our spiritual condition against these. If they are happy and considerate I am OK?

King Saul lost his love and reverence for the Lord: 1Sa 15:24 Then Saul said to Samuel, "I have sinned; I have indeed transgressed the command of the LORD and your words, because I feared the people and listened to their voice.

We see Saul referring to the Lord, when he speaks with Samuel, as "your Lord": 1Sa 15:30 Then he said, "I have sinned; *but* please honor me now before the elders of my people and before Israel, and go back with me, that I may worship the LORD your God." God is no more a personal God to him! Furthermore we see Saul worried about what others will think of him as king!!

Saul did some things right:

1Sa 15:13 And Samuel came to Saul, and Saul said to him, "Blessed are you of the LORD! I have carried out the command of the LORD."
1Sa 15:14 But Samuel said, "What then is this bleating of the sheep in my ears, and the lowing of the oxen which I hear?"

1Sa 15:15 And Saul said, "They have brought them from the Amalekites, for the people spared the best of the sheep and oxen, to sacrifice to the LORD your God; but the rest we have utterly destroyed."

He was supposed to destroy everything but decided himself what the Lord wills and spared some for sacrifice!! Cain also disobeyed the Lord and wanted to sacrifice fruit and vegetables instead of meat!! This was in fact a rebellion and likened to witchcraft.

After being called as king and with a humble heart (1Sa_9:21 And Saul answered and said, "Am I not a Benjamite, of the smallest of the tribes of Israel, and my family the least of all the families of the tribe of Benjamin? Why then do you speak to me in this way?"................) Saul is over time subtly influenced by the people, their adoration and worship, as he was a handsome man and stately in appearance. Pride sets in and we see Saul succumbing to the acknowledgements of men: 1Sa 15:12 And Samuel rose early in the morning to meet Saul; and it was told Samuel, saying, "Saul came to Carmel, and behold, he set up a monument for himself, then turned and proceeded on down to Gilgal."

The commandment to: (Deu_6:5 "and) you shall love the LORD your God with all your heart and with all your soul and with all your might was for a very specific reason. Without love there is no relationship! Without love it would be impossible to obey God!

In Eph 3 verses 17 to 19 we read that the love of God surpasses knowledge. Love compels us to know the depth, the height, width and breadth. Love compels us to go further. It is by His love we are filled up to all the fullness of God. If we are being led through life by a love for Christ we will be continually drawn to Him until we know His fullness. (Up to our capacity at any time)

In the New Covenant we have an even greater gift given to us. God not only calls us like Saul and David but dies for us. The result is staggeringly awesome: Joh 6:54 *"He who eats My flesh and drinks My blood has eternal life, and I will raise him up on the last day.* Joh 6:63 *"It is the Spirit who gives life; the flesh profits nothing; the words that I have spoken to you are spirit and are life"*. Joh 17:26 and *I have made Thy name known to them, and will make it known; that the love wherewith Thou didst love Me may be in them, and I in them."*

This love sacrifice of the Lord Jesus was done so that the love of God for us can be in us as He is in us!! The reward is eternal life and more, eternal life with God, with Jesus!! Joh 11:26 and everyone who lives and believes in Me shall never die. Do you believe this?"

I want to again refer you the reader to this passage of scripture: Joh 17:26 and *I have made Thy name known to them, and will make it known; that the love wherewith Thou didst love Me may be in them, and I in them."*

As the "star" in His hand (Rev 1 v 16) you my brother are to be a shining example of His love by experiencing His love and allowing His love to guide and direct you. Everything you do must be from this position of loving Him first. You have to: Joh 6:54 *"He who eats My flesh and drinks My blood has eternal life, and I will raise him up on the last day"*.

Not loving God first is a sin

The truth is that not loving God FIRST is a sin, otherwise why ask them to "REPENT"

Charles Spurgeon had a lot to say about sin:

Quote:

There was never an ill word spoken, nor an ill thought conceived, nor an evil deed done, for which God will not have punishment from some one or another. He will either have satisfaction from you, or else from Christ. If you have no atonement to bring through

Christ, you must for ever live paying the debt which you never can pay, in eternal misery; for as surely as God is God, He will sooner lose His Godhead than suffer one sin to go unpunished, or one particle of rebellion unrevenged. [Spurgeon, "Particular Redemption"]

Every "particle of rebellion" must be punished. God would not be God if he did not punish sin. This is a crucial point in the doctrine of the atonement. Many will say, "God is love! He will forgive everyone!" Not so! Forgiveness is not possible without punishment for sin. The dilemma, then, is if every sin must be punished, that would seem to indicate that no one can be saved! Thirdly, the answer to the dilemma is the heart of the atonement, namely, the substitution of Christ. Our sin, in fact, the world's sin must be placed on Christ if anyone will be forgiven of the infinite offense of sin. This is what Spurgeon believed. This is what made his preaching and ministry so powerful in the lives of many people.

One can almost hear his thunderous voice preaching the next words in one of his sermons:

Oh! then, beloved, think how great must have been the substitution of Christ, when it satisfied God for all the sins of His people. *For man's sin God demands eternal punishment; and God hath prepared a Hell into which He casts those who die impenitent. Oh! my brethren, can ye think what must have been the greatness of the atonement which was the substitution for all this agony which God would have cast upon us, if He had not poured it upon Christ. [Spurgeon, "Particular Redemption"]*

The agony that the sins of the elect deserved was placed on Christ. He was punished as if he were guilty of the sin that another committed. Such grace is incalculable and indescribable! But this is only part of the answer to the question of, "how can I be forgiven of sin?" For, in order for a substitution of guilt to take place, the person on whom the guilt will be placed must be a perfect man, otherwise the sacrifice is void. However, all men have sinned! Therefore, God the Son had to become a man and die. "But turn aside and see this great sight!—an incarnate God upon the cross; a substitute atoning for mortal guilt; a sacrifice satisfying the vengeance of heaven, and delivering the rebellious sinner."
End Quote

"Repent therefore or else I will come and remove your lampstand....."

No theology or religious activity is of any worth without obedience to this commandment: (Deu_6:5 "and) you shall love the LORD your God with all your heart and with all your soul and with all your might.

Do you want to be a spiritual, godly influence in these last days for the Lord? Then repent of lovelessness, confess your lack of first loving Him and come again to the cross of Calvary where He will "raise you up" again. Let Him truly be your Alpha and Omega, your beginning and your end. Repent of the spirit of Saul and recommit yourself to love Him and Him only first!!

Joh 21:15 - 17 So *when they had finished breakfast, Jesus *said to Simon Peter, "Simon, son of John, do you love Me more than these?" He *said to Him, "Yes, Lord; You know that I love You." He *said to him, "Tend My lambs." He *said to him again a second time, "Simon, son of John, do you love Me?" He *said to Him, "Yes, Lord; You know that I love You." He *said to him, "Shepherd My sheep." He *said to him the third time, "Simon, son of John, do you love Me?" Peter was grieved because He said to him the third time, "Do you love Me?" And he said to Him, "Lord, You know all things; You know that I love You." Jesus *said to him, "Tend My sheep.*

We see here that love is the essence of a relationship with Him. The Lord restores the most important spiritual condition in the human heart, love for God! David organises a 24/7 choir and worship before the Ark, the Presence of God!! And it is the FIRST thing he did when the Ark returns.

The first letter (Rev. 2) to the Churches is about love!!! Someone, I think it was the Beatles, wrote a song that said…"what has love got to do with it…." How about everything!!

Chris Hamman

THE BEGINNING

This last chapter is not the "end" but the beginning as the Lord will surely add to it as He deems fit for each who have come to this point in the book. The Lord is saying......:

(Extracts from Make Haste My Beloved- Frances Roberts)
Page 46
My wisdom and My love and My holiness are all working together with My saving power to bring you to perfection. My church is dear to My heart, or have you forgotten that you are Mine? Have you lost sight of the fact that you were created by My Spirit? Shall I not perfect all that I begin?

Page 32
I have waited for you with patience, but I beg you to turn to Me speedily, for truly the hour is late and much remains unfinished. Make a new commitment and I will bestow a fresh anointing and we shall rejoice together beyond anything in the past. Rise up, for the labourers are few.

I plead with you My people, to seek Me with intensity, with a broken, teachable spirit. I am not asking for your help but for your consecration. I need trumpets through which to sound, vessels through which to flow, hearts through which to love and lips that will honour My name!!

Grace is My empowering presence within you that enables you to become the person that I see when I look at you. Beloved, I can only see Jesus in you and you in Him. This is so exciting for Me. I absolutely love the fact that every time I look at you I see Him. When you are doing well and learning properly I see Him.

When you are doing badly and learning, I still see Him and I respond to Him in you! That is a grace that is rich towards you. (Graham Cooke)

Grace be with you for ever more!

REFERENCE MATERIAL

Index of some of the books and articles that assisted and influenced me and from which I quoted specific paragraphs:

BIBLES

New American Standard Bible......... Holman Bible Publishers Nashville

KJV ... from the E-Sword online application.

ARTICLES

Cheryl McGrath.............. www.greatsouthland.org.

Elaine Tavolacci .... www.awordinseason@live.com ... 2010

David Wilkerson............. February 8, 1988

Dave Kraft ....Today's Topical Bible

BOOKS

Created for Influence........................... William B Ford III

History Makers...................... William Ford III and Dutch Sheets

A Message to the Glorious Church....... Rick Joyner

Occult Invasion" (of the church), Dave Hunt, (ISBN 1-56507-831-4 dated 3 April 2005)

God's Will Our Dwelling Place............. Andrew Murray

Baptism In The Holy Spirit.................... Derek Prince

The Miracle of the Scarlet Thread .... Richard Booker

Whatever Happened to Worship.......... AW Tozer

Make Haste My Beloved .... Frances Roberts

ANNEXURE A

Making an Idol of Ministry
By Dave Kraft

Henri Nouwen once said that the main obstacle to loving God is service for God. This is ministry idolatry—not agreeing with Jesus that he has the rightful first place in our affections. Ministry idolatry is becoming increasingly widespread in evangelical Christianity in America, reaching epidemic proportions. It is showcased at network and denominational gatherings, where the focus and conversation is often not about Jesus but about us and what we are accomplishing and achieving. Leaders discuss the

"Idolatry creep" sneaks up on you because you can easily and quickly justify it by saying that everything you do is for the Lord, believing your motives are pure. We recognize this in businessmen who work obscene hours while insisting they do it all to benefit the family, when in reality it's all about them.

latest poster children for ministry success and their methods so we can all emulate them, buy their books, and attend their "how we did it" seminars and conferences.

Leaders must guard against ministry becoming a mistress. A mistress is someone who takes the place that only your wife should occupy. Ministry must never take the place of Jesus himself in your heart and in your values. As 1 John 5:21 says, "Little children, keep yourselves from idols." The New Living Translation says, "Dear children, keep away from anything that might take God's place in your hearts." Our hearts are idol factories, and ministry, for many leaders, is the king of idols

"Idolatry creep" sneaks up on you because you can easily and quickly justify it by saying that everything you do is for the Lord, believing your motives are pure. We recognize this in businessmen who work obscene hours while insisting they do it all to benefit the family, when in reality it's all about them.

Leaders must guard against ministry becoming a mistress. A mistress is someone who takes the place that only your wife should occupy. Ministry must never take the place of Jesus himself in your heart and in your values. As 1 John 5:21 says, "Little children, keep yourselves from idols." The New Living Translation says, "Dear children, keep away from anything that might take God's place in your hearts." Our hearts are idol factories, and ministry, for many leaders, is the king of idols.

We can start to rely on ministry instead of Jesus to meet deep needs in our own lives. I am convinced that many people move into leadership roles because of people needing them or because being in control satisfies something missing in their own sense of value or worth. I remember John Maxwell once saying, "If you need people you can lead people." One leader told me that the motivation for "his call" to ministry was the opportunity to resolve the problem of his own insecurities and feel better about himself. The Devil is out to snare Christian leaders, rendering them "ineffective or unfruitful" (2 Peter 1:8), and if he can't achieve his purposes through obvious sin, he will achieve them by taking something that is admirable and good and turning it on its ear to cause us to stumble.

The apostle Peter, in his insightful chapter to leaders, says, "Be sober-minded; be watchful. Your adversary the devil prowls around like a roaring lion, seeking someone to devour" (1 Peter 5:8). Our enemy can devour us through ministry by letting the ministry itself replace Jesus in our affections. Unfortunately, we are often quicker to recognize this happening in others than in our own lives.

I began my ministry with the Navigators in 1968 and enjoyed thirty-eight years of ministry with them before retiring in 2005 to come on staff at Mars Hill Church in Seattle. During my first few years with the Navigators, I began my drift into ministry idolatry. I had one of my first wake-up calls (I needed several of these before I could truly see what was going on in my life) in a visit with Tommy Adkins, who was a Nav+

4 staffer, friend, and mentor to me.

I had just finished a good visit with Tommy, and we were walking to my car parked in his driveway. Tommy had piercing blue eyes, and I was about to personally experience their piercing quality. When we got to my car, he said he wanted to share something with me. "This can't be good," I thought to myself.

Tommy grabbed a sheet from the notebook he was carrying and laid it on the hood of my VW. He then drew out an illustration that is familiar to all Navigators—the wheel. In the center of the wheel was Jesus. Tommy focused those blue eyes on me and asked the heart-stopping question, "Dave, what is in the center of your wheel [your life]?" I quickly told him that it was Jesus, to which he replied, "I don't think so."

Tommy asked if he could write what he perceived was the center of "my wheel," to which I answered yes. He then slowly wrote the word "men." In the Navigators, finding and giving yourself to faithful men was the centerpiece of our ministry philosophy. Founder Dawson Trotman, in a classic message he preached, asked, "Men, where is your man? . . . Women, where is your woman? Where is the man or the woman who is living today for Jesus Christ because of your life?"

Having men in the place of where Jesus should be was ministry idolatry—plain and simple and painful to admit. The good had become the idol in my life—not noticed by me but by Tommy. He was absolutely right! As we sing in a classic hymn: "Prone to wander, Lord, I feel it, prone to leave the God I love." Even today this sin is crouching in the dark waiting to devour me. I am not actually leaving the God I love, but rather I am tempted to push him to a marginalized place and put ministry in the center of my life, instead of keeping Christ enthroned there.

It is not my intention to give some kind of formula in dealing with each of the mistakes addressed in this book. There are no "four easy steps to deal with ministry idolatry." But I do want to share some things I am learning about dealing with each of the mistakes leaders make. Let me state again that I have made all these mistakes myself, and I have seen people in ministries, organizations, groups, and churches that I have been associated with make them.

So, how have I dealt with ministry idolatry?

For me the first step is realizing that this is a problem for me. I deeply desire to want to confess and repent when this sin comes to my attention, as opposed to making excuses and rationalizing. It should grieve my soul that I am allowing something to take the place of Jesus in my heart and affections. Like King David, I want to pray, "Against you, you only, have I sinned" (Psalms 51:4). My primary sin here is against God!

Most every day I make the issue of ministry idolatry a matter of prayer, asking for the power of Jesus through the Holy Spirit to occupy center stage in my life. For me, I find that ministry idolatry is an attitude, a mind-set, as opposed to an action. It begins with the way I look at things, the way I think.

Colossians 3:4 is helpful to me: "When Christ who is your life appears, then you will also appear with him in glory." Jesus is my life—not ministry, success, converts, disciples, developing leaders, being respected by my peers, etc. I need to keep being reminded of this truth. Paul says in Philippians 1:21, "For to me to live is Christ, and to die is gain." For me to live is Christ, not someone else or something else. I have several passages of Scripture memorized (in addition to those just mentioned) on ministry idolatry, including 1 John 5:21 and Revelation 2:4.

The Lord uses these Scriptures to get my attention and point out my sin. This is one reason I want to be consistent in my time in Scripture: to allow him to speak to my sinful heart. We used to say in the Navigators that God's Word will keep you from sin, or sin will keep you from God's Word. Regularly reviewing key verses, meditating on them, and praying over them helps a good deal.

When the Lord makes it clear that I am starting to drift, I want to immediately own it, repent, confess, and ask for his help in agreeing with him that he is central. I want to be especially sensitive to others in my family or on the teams I am a part of when they bring this sin to my attention. One of my life values is to immediately respond to God's revealed truth, whether that truth comes directly to me through Scripture or through the rebuke of a family or team member.

Using the story of a fictitious church team to demonstrate the problems, principles, and practice of finding solutions, leadership expert Dave Kraft uncovers the top 10 critical mistakes leaders make and shows you how to avoid them so you can have ministry and relationships that last.

ANEXURE B

CHOSEN

Barnes' Commentary on John 15:16

Ye have not chosen me - The word here translated "chosen" is that from which is derived the word "elect," and means the same thing. It is frequently thus translated, Mark 13:20; Matthew 24:22, Matthew 24:24, Matthew 24:31; Colossians 3:12. It refers here, doubtless, to his choosing or electing them to be apostles. He says that it was not because they had chosen him to be their teacher and guide, but because he had designated them to be his apostles. See John 6:70; also Matthew 4:18-22. He thus shows them that his love for them was pure and disinterested; that it commenced when they had no affection for him; that it was not a matter of obligation on his part, and that therefore it placed them under more tender and sacred obligations to be entirely devoted to his service. The same may be said of all who are endowed with talents of any kind, or raised to any office in the church or the state. It is not that they have originated these talents, or laid God under obligation. What they have they owe to his sovereign goodness, and they are bound to devote all to his service. Equally true is this of all Christians. It was not that by nature they were more inclined than others to seek God, or that they had any native goodness to recommend them to him, but it was because he graciously inclined them by his Holy Spirit to seek him; because, in the language of the Episcopal and Methodist articles of religion, "The grace of Christ prevented them;" that is, went before them, commenced the work of their personal salvation, and thus God in sovereign mercy chose them as His own. Whatever Christians, then, possess, they owe to God, and by the most tender and sacred ties they are bound to be his followers.

ANNEXURE C

THE JEWISH CONNECTION

For he is not a Jew who is one outwardly, nor is circumcision that which is outward in the flesh. But he is a Jew who is one inwardly; and circumcision is that which is of the heart, by the Spirit, not by the letter; and his praise is not from men, but from God. (Rom 2:28,29)

The church is not a replacement of the original chosen generation, Israel, but a fulfilment of the Lord's plan and design. In the above passage the statement "by the Spirit" provides the key to the new dispensation we understand to be the new testament or covenant.

The commentaries explain that the name *Yehudah* shares the same root as the Hebrew word *hoda'ah,* which means acknowledgement or submission. One who acknowledges G-d's existence and submits to His authority—to the extent that he is willing to sacrifice his life for the sanctification of His name—he is called a *Yehudi (Jew).*

ANNEXURE D

THE TESTIMONY of Belma Vardy

Belma has a very effective dance and worship ministry. Travelling extensively, she works with adults, teens, and children of many different denominations, teaching them how to know a greater intimacy and freedom with God. She has produced four worship dance videos: God's Children in a Celebration of Dance, Discipling Children in Worship Dance, Devotional Dance, and Lets Dance!

In *Catch the Fire,* I (Belma) shared some of my testimony of the ways in which I experienced the power of God's love in my life. There were many other things taking place that I did not, and at the time could not, convey. It is an honour and a privilege to be able to share more of God's grace in my life in these few pages.

For weeks I had been going to the meetings at the Airport Vineyard. All around me, people were manifesting the Spirits presence and power in all sorts of ways, but nothing seemed to be happening to me. I wanted so badly to have what the others were getting. I prayed and prayed. Nothing happened. I was really starting to feel quite strange about this. I started to ask God questions. "What was wrong with me? Why aren't You touching *me*? Have You forgotten about me?" I would sit quiet as a mouse at the meetings and just take it all in, sometimes really focussing in on some of the manifestations. I continued to come to the meetings, watching, waiting, and wondering. One evening during worship, I just hung my head and prayed in tongues. All of a sudden, I felt something that can only be described as a liquid heat rise up from the inside of me, and through all the music and singing I heard

God's Voice in a loud whisper saying, "I want you to worship Me. I want you to seek Me."

I raised my hands and felt His Presence wrap around me. I repented for not seeking Him first, but rather the manifestations. That night I discovered some of what it means to meet God face to Face.

The next day I was walking through a department store. At the same time, I was praying quietly under my breath, thanking the Lord for the intimate time of worship we had enjoyed together the night before. All of a sudden I found myself in the middle of the store's toy section. My instinct was to run, as I had wanted to many times before. But instead, I found myself glued to the floor. I stood in silence and looked around. I was shocked! I realized my heart wasn't reeling. The deep ache I'd carried for seven long years was gone! I gasped in amazement. Tears started to roll down my face.

I need to explain a bit of my past. After twelve years of marriage, my husband walked out on me. That devastated me, ripped apart my emotions, and left me feeling crushed, brokenhearted, and overcome with grief. I was even more wasted when, a few months after he left, I found out that he was living with another woman, and that she was carrying his baby! This completely did me in. Hopelessness, despair, and anxiety-filled days were followed by lonely nights with endless hours of weeping. The hurt took deep root, and eventually became anger; the anger became bitterness, and a dark depression set in.

Different fantasies would run through my mind. For a while, I wanted to kill my ex-husband and his girlfriend, Noreen,[5] kidnap their baby and run away. That was supposed to be *my* baby.

When I heard they were having another child, I felt I was on the edge of a nervous breakdown. I shuddered whenever Noreen came to mind; the anger and hate became stronger, and tormented me for almost six years.

It was for these reasons that I had such a hard time in a toy store. Baby clothes, baby toys, diapers, etc.— they all stirred up a hurt that was just too deep to bear.
But here I found myself standing in the middle of this toy section. This time there was *no* pain, *no* heartache, *no* sadness. I asked myself, "Where did all that stuff go?? It's gone!" The realization dawned that no one but the Lord could bring this healing. This was truly a miracle of God! He had completely washed away all my pain.
As I stood there glued to the floor, I started to thank Him and praise Him, and as I did so, I felt joy bubble up from the inside of me. That same feeling of liquid heat poured all over me again, bringing with it a feeling of total peace. The thought came to me, "Lord I want to follow only You and what You have for me. You may have purposed the shaking or laughing for others, but for me You choose to work differently, and I accept that."

A number of days went by. As I was having my devotions and praying in the Spirit, I felt a longing to pray for Noreen. This really shocked me, and I found it very strange as I had never done that before. But I was feeling a love and compassion for her that I knew could come only from the Lord. As I started to pray for her, these feelings became stronger and more real. Again I felt that liquid heat!

Over the next few days, I continued to feel compelled to pray for Noreen, and at one point, I heard a whisper. It seemed to come from the inner depth of my soul. But it also seemed to fill the room. The voice said, "Call Noreen." At first I thought I was imagining it. I continued to pray, this time in tongues, trying to ignore the voice. It became louder and I felt it tugging at my heart. I thought, "This *can't* be."
I waited. Two weeks went by. I did not call. But the tug on my heart continued, and it wouldn't go away. I just could not get up enough nerve to call. I rehearsed my excuses, and the

best I could come up with was "What could I possibly say to her?" One morning, while wrestling all this through again in prayer, the Lord answered back, "I will give you the words. Trust Me."

A month later, I was praying again—and felt myself being overcome by His Presence. I picked up the telephone and dialled. I started feeling very nervous and wanted to get off the line before she picked up. Noreen came on the telephone, and I didn't identify myself, but just shared with her some things that were on my heart. Noreen listened and then she thanked me. I was about to hang up when she said, "Wait! Do you know how I can get hold of Belma?" I felt myself tightening up and very curtly asked, "Why?" Noreen answered, "Because I have got to tell her I am so sorry!"

I felt my heart completely soften and melt. Tears rolled down my face. Suddenly I felt the Presence of the Lord even more intensely, as if He was flowing through the telephone wires. I identified myself to Noreen, and the conversation that followed lasted for three and a half hours that night! We spoke again the next day for another three hours! We called each other for the next two weeks almost every day. I felt a love and compassion for this woman that I knew could only come from God. She was now alone with her children and was struggling to make ends meet. I was able to share my faith in God with her. Another miracle from God.

Four weeks went by, and though I stopped calling, I continued to pray for Noreen on a daily basis. Once again I felt a tug on my heart. During one of my prayer times, I saw what the Lord wanted me to do next. In my spirit, I saw a picture of my car filled with groceries and clothes and toys for Noreen and her children. I believed that this picture could only be from God, so I proceeded getting busy shopping. It took six weeks to get all the things together. I felt totally led by love to do this. I prayed over every item and every article. When it was all ready, I called Noreen and arranged to meet with her.

We met on a Sunday morning in a church parking lot. At first it felt extremely awkward and we both seemed quite nervous. I prayed under my breath. Suddenly I felt the heat again, and I sensed the Presence of the Lord with us. From that moment on I felt an atmosphere of total peace and I knew that this time together was in God's perfect will! I then asked Noreen to open up her trunk. I started to fill it with groceries. Noreen began adding up the dollar value of the bags and said, "I'm going to have to pay you back for all of this." I said, "No, I don't want you to pay it back. Just receive it as a gift." The bags continued to go into her trunk until it was completely filled. Noreen then started to help me load more bags into the back seat of her car and then the front seat, until the car was so full we couldn't get another thing in. Noreen started to cry and said, "No one has ever done anything like this for me before. Why are *you* doing it?" I answered her, "Because it's in my heart to do." She asked, "But what will I tell my children?" I answered, "Just tell them that God cares for them." Noreen just shook her head and said, "I feel like I'm in another world."

We ended up talking in the parking lot for an hour—the first time we'd spoken face to face. Towards the end of that time, I gave Noreen a Christian video for her children, and then we said our good-byes. I felt her heart open as she gave me a long, eight-second hug. I felt like we were surrounded and immersed in so much love. The love of Jesus.

As I drove away, prayers of thanksgiving gushed forth for miracle after miracle. All of a sudden I felt a heat fill the car, and then, in my spirit, I saw a picture.
Noreen, her children, and I were standing in the throne room of God in front of the Father. Jesus was standing behind us, with His Arms on both our shoulders and what looked like wings of protection hovering over the children. I clearly heard a loud whisper fill my car as He said, "Those children do not belong to Noreen, they belong to Me. And whatsoever you have done to them, you have done to Me." I

started to weep and intercede for their salvation. I knew that God had His Hand on them.

God has healed and restored my broken heart. He has washed away my grief, hopelessness, and despair, my anger and bitterness, and He has replaced it all with His unconditional love and His peace. I know that when we harbour anger and bitterness, we only destroy ourselves and put up walls that keep us from receiving from God. I have found that as I respond in prayer, and in trusting obedience walk out the desires of God's heart, the walls I have put up start slowly collapsing. As they come down, I'm far more able to hear a lot more clearly from God. It has been a privilege and an honour that God used me in this way to show my forgiveness and God's Love towards Noreen.

ANNEXURE E

Chris Hamman

ROOM 405
Full Gospel Business Men's convention in Atlantic City
Rev. John Sherrill

Of all the variety of experience with the Holy Spirit, one thing held true in every case. Whether the Baptism came quietly or with a bang, unexpectedly or after long seeking, the ultimate result was to draw the individual closer to Christ. Jesus was no longer a figure on the pages of a history book. Nor, even, a memory from some personal mountain-top experience. His Spirit was with the Baptized believer in a present-time, minute-by-minute way, showing him at every turn the nature and personality of Christ

And suddenly I realized that I had come full cycle.

This whole search had begun in the vacuum that had followed my own mountain-top experience in the hospital. I was following—perhaps all Christians follow—the path the disciples took: First, there was a direct, personal encounter with Christ. Then, He appears to go away. There is a longing for His return, and a helplessness, because nothing we do seems to bring that return.

Wasn't the lesson I had learned from the Bible, and from the people who had had the experience today, that in order to see Him again we need the mediation of the Holy Spirit? "But when your Advocate has come, whom I will send you from the Father—the Spirit of truth that issues from the Father—he will bear witness to me." [8]

THERE SEEMS TO BE a strange link between taking a seemingly foolish step—which God specifies—and receiving spiritual power. Moses stretched his rod over the water at Jehovah's command and the Red Sea divided. The penniless widow was instructed, through Elisha, to collect many vessels and to start pouring oil into them from her small jar: when the widow had finished obeying she had collected enough oil to pay all her debts. Elijah had to strike the water with his mantle before it would part.

I once had occasion to talk about this phenomenon with Billy Graham. He had noticed it for years, and was of the opinion that the secret lay in overcoming self-consciousness and self-will sufficiently to perform the task. It was extremely difficult, he had found, for most people to get out of their seats and walk forward to the altar rail at one of his meetings. But he had also observed that the seemingly foolish gesture brought power with it.

For many people speaking in tongues falls into the same category. It seems to them pointless and embarrassing. In these people, no doubt, the final yielding of their tongues produces a deep religious experience. But this was not the point at which my own resistance came. I could see by now some of the logic behind tongues: I could imagine myself praising God in a language I could not understand; I could imagine myself praying for someone in tongues if I could not imagine how to pray for them with my understanding. By now, in fact, I was becoming increasingly eager to receive the Baptism in the Holy Spirit and it seemed fairly likely to me that tongues would be a part of it.

No, the point of resistance for me lay in a different quarter. There was one act which many of the Pentecostals performed which I was not going to do. They would stand up,
raise both hands toward heaven, and shout "Praise the Lord!"

I knew that the practice was a very old one in the Judeo-Christian tradition:

> Because thy loving kindness is better than life,
> My lips shall praise thee.
> So will I bless thee while I live:
> I will lift up my hands in thy name.
> My soul shall be satisfied as with marrow and fatness;
> And my mouth shall praise thee with joyful lips.[1]

I knew that "Praise the Lord" was a favorite phrase of the psalmists, and was even part of the liturgy or my own well-mannered Episcopal service.

Nevertheless, the practice as the Pentecostals did it was objectionable to me. No doubt each person draws the line somewhere...

December 2, 1960. It was the date of the opening of the Full Gospel Business Men's convention in Atlantic City to which Tib and I had agreed to go, back in the spring, so many months ago. The meetings were being held at The President, one of the large on-the-water hotels. Friday night we registered, went for a walk on the cold, moonlit beach and turned in early.

I don't know why I was so unprepared for the emotions of the breakfast meeting next morning. I'd been to many Pentecostal gatherings by now, but never to such a large one: early in the morning several hundred men and women crowded into The President's grand ballroom. They ate rapidly, then pushed their chairs back in obvious anticipation of something to follow.

On the platform at the end of the room sat two dozen business and professional men. Some, I was told, had flown across the country to attend the meetings; one had come in his own private plane.

While we were finishing our coffee, one of these men stood up and called out the name of a song. Everyone joined in, loud, lusty and wonderful as I'd heard it before among Pentecostals. By the middle of the second song a woman at the next table was weeping. There was nothing especially emotional about the song itself, it was one of the standard old Gospel hymns, "When I Survey the Wondrous Cross." But crying seems to be as infectious as laughter. Soon some of the men on the platform were unabashedly bringing out their handkerchiefs. What was it that swept a room this way? I felt it too; so did Tib sitting next to me. Both of us were studiously avoiding looking the other one in the eye.

As the music continued, several people at the tables began to sing "in the Spirit." Soon the whole room was singing a complicated harmony-without-score, created^spontaneously. It was eerie but extraordinarily beautiful. The song leader was no longer trying to direct the music, but let the melodies create themselves: without prompting one quarter of the room would suddenly start to sing very loudly while others subsided. Harmonies and counterharmonies wove in and out of each other.

By now tears were flowing without restraint all around the room. A weathered, stonefaced man near us raised calloused hands and sang out, "Praise the Lord!" An elderly woman two tables away stood up and began to dance a little jig. She looked like a great-grandmother, dressed in black with her white hair in a bun. No one paid her the slightest attention. Except me, that is; I couldn't take my eyes off her. And as I watched, a phenomenon occurred which I have still not been able to explain. It was very hot in the ballroom, perhaps 85 degrees. Yet while grandmother danced I distinctly saw, against the dark velvet curtains of the room, soft billows of visible "breath" coming from her mouth as if she were standing outside in the cold.

The effect on me of watching these manifestations is hard to describe. Instead of being embarrassed or feeling that I was watching something unseemly, I had the overall feeling that this was wholesome and good, and I remembered Dr. Van Dusen's remark that Pentecostal exuberance was "ultimately healthy."

And then suddenly it was all over. The singing stopped; the mood of the meeting shifted. People brought out handkerchiefs and dried their eyes. A California dairyman named Demos Shakarian, who is the Fellowship's president, stepped to the center of the platform and conducted the business end of the meeting It was over in five minutes, and as the weary veteran of many treasurer's reports I was filled with gratitude.

A prayer followed. The "breakfast" meeting lasted for four hours. There was preaching and more singing. There was a period during which people from the floor could tell about some experience with the Holy Spirit. I noticed that several in the audience, when introducing themselves, confirmed what Charles Maurice had told us: there were others in the ballroom who were not Pentecostals by denomination, they were Episcopalians, Methodists, Baptists, Presbyterians, Lutherans. When at last the meeting adjourned for lunch, Dr. William Reed, a surgeon and an Episcopal lay reader whom we'd known for some years, came over to Tib and me and asked us to join a group who were having sandwiches sent to one of the rooms upstairs. The room they had chosen was to become strangely important to me: Room 405.

The door to Room 405 was slightly ajar when we arrived fifteen minutes later, so I knocked and we walked in, wondering who would be there. Sitting with his back to the window which framed the rolling, pounding Atlantic Ocean, was Jim Brown, a Presbyterian minister from Pennsylvania. Bill Reed was on the sofa, talking to a Methodist woman minister from Philadelphia, Olivia Henry. And out in the kitchen making coffee were an Episcopalian social worker named Dorothy Randall and Jim s wire, Marianne. There was not, I noted, a Pentecostal among us.

Tib sat down beside Jim with her back to the Atlantic. The conversation centered on the morning's meeting, the different people who had spoken, the points of view expressed. It was several minutes before I noticed that Tib was not joining in.
Sandwiches arrived from the coffee shop downstairs, and the talk turned to more personal subjects: the needs and hopes that each of us there hi the room had brought to the convention. From time to time I looked across at Tib. She sat withdrawn and silent, the sandwich on her plate untouched. She'd said nothing about feeling bad that morning, but there was a weariness about her posture now—as though she held a tremendous weight on her shoulders, all alone.

All at once she stood up. She murmured something about having to make a phone call and before I could stop her, she was gone.

Something very strange was going on with all of this. Tib and I, alike in so many respects, were especially alike in one area. We were proud of our objectivity. We were then, and still are, of the opinion that objectivity and honesty are closely related. If you looked at a scene with many eyes, we believed, you were more likely to see it whole.

But objectivity also served another function for us: it acted as a shield. We were not by nature joiners or true-believers. We did not like to be identified with a group. And at the same time by profession and by instinct we really were interested in other people's enthusiasms. By keeping about us a spirit of objectivity, remaining always interested observers, but never committed participants, we were defended from the pressures of joining every group we wrote about.

I had made one major exception to this rule when I be came a Christian. And with that experience I discovered a flaw in the principle of objectivity. Before I made my own commitment I thought of myself as viewing Christianity from as many vantage points as possible, thus getting an accurate view. What I did not realize was that this very objectivity was itself a block to seeing the whole picture. Because it effectively cut off one essential viewpoint: the view from the inside.

For many months now I had been looking at the Baptism in the Holy Spirit from as many angles as possible: all from the outside. I had decided with my intellect that this was a valid Christian experience. Now I wanted to explore it from the inside. Tib had followed most of the research and interviews. She was interested: but still only as an observer. I think now that when she left Room 405 she knew what she was doing. She was deliberately taking with her our burden of objectivity. She was making it possible for me to step inside an experience, taking defenses out the door with her.

Of course at the time I realized all of this only on the most subliminal of levels. I doubted that she had a telephone call to make; I knew that something was weighing on her; I sensed that she did not want me to follow her. In some mystic way she was to play a tremendous role in the event that followed, because she took with her our cherished outsider's look, while I was left free to participate in the shock and jolt of experience.

And yet leaving the room, she did not leave me, for we were mysteriously linked together during the next hours. When Tib left 405, she'd gone outside to walk on the boardwalk. After a while she stepped down onto the sand where she could walk right at the water's edge. She walked for a long, long time. The sun sank lower in the sky. Facing south as she was, her eyes began to be bothered by it. Tib had always been extremely light-sensitive, choosing chairs that looked away from windows and so forth. She started to turn around and head north with her back to the sun when a sentence popped into her mind with the force of a command.

"Look neither to the right nor to the left, but only straight ahead."

But straight ahead was the dazzling sun. She walked on a little farther, squinting her eyes. It was getting late. She was a long way from the hotel by now. The meeting in Room 405 must be over, she thought: I would be looking for her. But each time she started to turn around and retrace her steps, the extraordinary words reappeared in her mind.

"Neither right nor left. Only straight ahead."

The sun was lower still. Glittering on the waves, glaring straight into her eyes. And still Tib walked on, into the bunding light....

In 405 there was a certain air of expectancy. There were six of us now, seated in a casual circle about the room. Several people had related instances of the power of Spirit-filled prayer, and someone now suggested that we pray this way for the problems on our minds.

Partly in an effort to overcome self-consciousness, I shut my eyes. Soon I'd lost track of who was talking in the room. Someone began to pray in the Spirit. It was a woman's voice, but I did not know whose. In fact, from that moment on I lost contact with individuals. It was as if the separate personalities had disappeared and a single individual, talking in various timbres and accents had taken their place. Minds seemed to work together: a sentence would be started by one person and finished by another.

Now someone else began to pray in tongues. Another started to sing very softly in the Spirit. I felt my throat tighten, as it had downstairs at the height of the singing. I suppose I was crying, deeply, silently. Slowly I began to lose my own identity too, until finally self-awareness disappeared.

This is quite an experience, losing consciousness of self. And I was helped by gaining, at the same time, the awareness that another Presence was in the room. And suddenly He was there again, in light as I had seen Him in the hospital. But this time -the light blazed through my closed lids, blinding, dizzying, fearful. I was afraid of this approaching contact. I tried to pull my mind away from it, to concentrate on the solid room around me and the human beings in it
"Look neither to the right nor to the left, but only straight ahead."

The voice came from behind me. I thought it was Olivia Henry's but I have never been sure. Just at the moment when I was about to take refuge in self-consciousness, it pulled me back to the center. Several times more, in the next hour, the command was repeated, always just in time to prevent my attention from being sidetracked. I never knew whether the words were meant for me or not, but they performed an immeasurable service. They kept me from being distracted by what was going on to either side, from being conscious of how I looked and what other people thought of me; they brought me back always to the blinding light directly ahead.

There was a lull in the praying and singing. The voices around me receded into a quiet murmur.
A man's voice: "I believe John wants the Baptism in the Spirit."

I felt, more than saw, the five people rise and form a circle around me.

What happened next is due in large part to the role Tib was playing as she walked along up the beach toward the sun. I believe that, although I am unable to explain it. Without this help from her I would hardly have run the strange new danger of totally new experience.

At the time, there in Room 405, nothing of this was going through my mind. Just the opposite: the very nature of that hour was pure experience, with a maximum of allowing to happen what was going to happen, and a minimum of analysis.

The group moved closer around me. It was almost as if (hey were forming with their bodies a funnel through which was concentrated the flow of the Spirit that was pulsing through that room. It flowed into me as I sat there, listening to the Spirit-song around me. Now the tongues swelled to a crescendo, musical and lovely. I opened my mouth, wondering if I too could join in, but nothing happened. I felt a numbness in my lips and a constriction in my throat And suddenly I had the impression that in order to speak in tongues I had only to look up. But this was a joyful gesture. All my training and inclination was to approach God with head bowed.

Strange that such a simple gesture as lifting the head should become a battleground. And soon—perhaps because I did not obey quick enough—another directive came clear: not only was I to lift my head but I was to lift my hands too, and I was to cry out with all the feeling in me a great shout of praise to God. A hot, angry flush rose and flooded me. It was the thing above all things that I didn't want to do.
Perhaps because it was so very repugnant to me the issue was clearly drawn as one of sheer obedience.

What other possible significance could there be in my raising my hands high and mouthing some words of praise? But that was what I had to do, and I knew it. Foolish as it seemed. Or maybe because it seemed foolish. I heard E. Stanley Jones saying, "I had to become God's fool."

With a sudden burst of will I thrust my hands into the air, turned my face full upward, and at the top of my voice I shouted:

"Praise the Lord!"

It was the floodgate opened. From deep inside me, deeper than I knew voice could go, came a torrent of joyful sound. It was not beautiful, like the tongues around me. I had the impression that it was ugly: explosive and grunting. I didn't care. It was healing it was forgiveness, it was love too deep for words and it burst from me in wordless sound. After that one shattering effort of will, my will was released, freed to soar into union with Him.

No further conscious effort was requited of me at all, not even choosing the syllables with which to express my joy. The syllables were all there, ready-formed for my use, more abundant than my earth-bound lips and tongue could give shape to.
It was not that I felt out of control of the situation: I had never felt more truly master of myself, more integrated and at peace with warring factions inside myself. I could stop the tongues at any instant, but who would? I wanted them never to stop. And so I prayed on, laughing and free, while the setting sun shone through the window, and the stars came out.

Chris Hamman

Chris Hamma

www.ingramcontent.com/pod-product-compliance
Lightning Source LLC
Chambersburg PA
CBHW052056110526
44591CB00013B/2234